P9-CJW-436

The New Cross-Country Ski Book

THE NEW
Cross-Country
Ski Book

8th EDITION

John Caldwell

THE STEPHEN GREENE PRESS
Lexington, Massachusetts

Copyright © John Caldwell, 1964, 1968, 1971, 1973, 1975, 1977, 1981, 1984, 1987
All rights reserved

This eighth edition first published in 1987 by The Stephen Greene Press, Inc.
Published simultaneously in Canada by Penguin Books Canada Limited.
Distributed by Viking Penguin Inc., 40 West 23rd Street, New York, NY 10010.

Publishing history of *The New Cross-Country Ski Book:*

The Cross-Country Ski Book, published in 1964
The Cross-Country Ski Book, 2nd Edition, published in 1968
The New Cross-Country Ski Book, 3rd Edition, published in 1971
The New Cross-Country Ski Book, 4th Edition, published in 1973
The New Cross-Country Ski Book, 4th Edition (indexed), published in 1975
Cross-Country Skiing Today, 5th Edition, published in 1977
The Cross-Country Ski Book, 6th Edition, published in 1981
The Cross-Country Ski Book, 7th Edition, published in 1984

Photo credits: A-Foto, Oslo, p. 5; American Birkebeiner Foundation, p. 8 (top);
Mike Brady, p. 139; Hep Caldwell, pp. 152 and 153; Tim Caldwell, p. 65;
Joan Eaton, Waterville Valley, pp. 147 and 157; Bob George, pp. 8 (bottom),
122, 154, and 155; Geordie Heller, pp. 50, 53, 105, 109–110; Jussi Kirjavainen, p. 2;
and M. Pietinen, p. 124. All other photos by the author.

Library of Congress Cataloging-in-Publication Data
Caldwell, John H.
  The new cross-country ski book.
  Includes index.
  1. Cross-country skiing. I. Title.
GV855.3.C35 1987   796.93   87-9992
ISBN 0-8289-0611-4

Designed by Joyce C. Weston
Set in Palatino and Zapf Chancery Medium Italic
by Publication Services, Inc.
Printed in the United States of America
by The Alpine Press, Inc.
Produced by Unicorn Production Services, Inc.

Except in the United States of America, this book is sold subject to the condition
that it shall not, by way of trade or otherwise, be lent, re-sold, hired out, or otherwise circulated without the publisher's prior consent in any form of binding or
cover other than that in which it is published and without a similar condition including this condition being imposed on the subsequent purchaser.

Contents

1

Introduction

*A*LL OF cross-country skiing is divided into three parts: the first is the history or background, the second part consists of stories and anecdotes that help to illustrate the first part, and the third part is where we are now. In this book I have paid attention to this. Each chapter contains approximately three parts. The first parts are history according to John Caldwell and therefore occasionally lacking in some people's perspective, but at least the reporting is accurate. The second parts contain occasional lies, but what stories don't? Sometimes the first and second parts are indistinguishable. The third parts are fairly current and will no doubt become rapidly outdated and have to be thrown back in with the first parts. That's the way this sport has been going.

I have more reasons than I have mentioned for doing all of this. Since I have started skiing, back in the '30s by chance and then seriously since the '40s, I've had a lot of good experiences and I want to recall some of them for you—thus the background and anecdotal parts of each chapter. In addition, I've found that historical events really do teach us a lot if we study them . . . the present administration in Washington excepted. They help to put things in perspective, and that's very important these days.

There is also a theme here with which many of you are familiar. It's the recurrence idea. With cars—do you think we will ever really settle in with all compacts, or all medium-sized cars, or with all those big babies? Chances are, no! With women's fashions and especially skirts, how many choices do they have from year to year? Long, medium long (maybe), medium short (maybe), short, and then?

1

While women's cross-country skiing did not catch on early in America, it was a fad in Finland during 1923, as can be seen here.

THE NEW
CROSS-COUNTRY
SKI BOOK

Changing styles sell. Anyone on Madison Avenue can tell you that. The result is that we often come back to a point where we've been before. In order to keep with this recurrence theme, I have copied the outline of the 1964 first edition, which contained a mere six chapters plus a little introduction. With one exception. The skating technique has brought on the most significant changes in cross-country skiing since the invention of the sport, so I'm going to add one more chapter, which concentrates on it.

Like some of the ol' Vermonters say in Town Meetings, when referring to the present school systems, if it was good enough for us back then, I guess it's good enough for you now. I say that to you about my first book.

During 1963 and 1964 when I wrote the first edition, I had to take pains to explain what cross-country (x-c) skiing was. I went into some detail on many other aspects of the sport then. Now, it's hardly necessary since there are several different books out that cover each of the topics I tried to handle in one chapter. I used to pride myself on possessing all the x-c books written in English. There were at least three of them then. Now I can't keep up with them.

A good friend of mine, Mike Brady, and I formed the AAABCCIE (which stands for the Association of American Authors of Books on Cross-Country in English) and we have yearly meetings to look over the field, so to speak. Like me, Mike also came out with his first book in the mid-'60s and we feel a certain amount of pride in having been the first authors to hit the stands. Mike has written much more than I and that's a good thing because under the rules of our association, I can steal any of his stuff. So occasionally I do. Thanks, Mike!

There are so many books, as I have said, and other publications that cover x-c exclusively, or at least in part, that you fans are really lucky. Cross-country skiers have to be the most prolific writers of any sportsmen in the world. And now, even lots of catalogs advertising ski equipment—like Tom Jacobs' Reliable Racing catalog—have all sorts of hints on ski-related topics. It reminds me of all the seed catalogs I get in the mail. There's an encyclopedia of information in them all taken together.

INTRODUCTION

Lilly Caldwell, neé Shuell, my daughter-in-law, and Zachary Caldwell, my nephew. These two posed for most of the technique shots, thus keeping things in the family.

So you don't need one more book on the basics, and in this one I am gleaning a few items from ideas I've had — ones I feel are good — presenting them, and using a lot more space on the history and anecdote sections.

Until very recently everyone who wrote or talked about technique had in mind the diagonal technique, complete with double-poling, herring-bones, step turns, and all that bit. Single stride and

Toini Gustafsson, double gold medal winner in the 1968 Olympics, starts a race in Oslo, Norway.

INTRODUCTION

single step were two terms often used also. Now all of this has been changed to being called the classical technique (or in some cases, classical techniques) in order to contrast it with the freestyle technique, which is primarily a skating technique used especially by racers. For your information, freestyle x-c technique is not the same as freestyle Alpine skiing, but is mainly skating. In freestyle races you may use the classical techniques anytime you want, but most of the gunners skate the whole course. In classical races you may skate only in designated sections, usually around corners.

If you know me, you can be sure you won't get bombarded with a lot of technical stuff in this book. I'm a guy that has carried the saying "If it works, don't fix it" one step further. If it works I'm not too interested in learning anymore about it—like the technicalities of certain ski constructions, or the chemical make-up of various bases, or why certain training effects take place, or why certain ski movements work better than others. Maybe I'm too easy to please.

Even though I've been teaching beginners since 1951, most of the stories in here are about the racing crowd and that's because my racing and coaching experiences have been so very memorable. Besides, the people associated with the racing scene are more fun to tease.

I've seen the competitors, and particularly the Americans, set almost all the present-day standards for every phase of x-c skiing and so it's clearly important to have this background. Tourskiers are lucky to have so many guinea pigs out there testing techniques, waxes, equipment, clothing, snow compaction, and anything else associated with the sport. This book is dedicated to all my friends who have had a hand in this development.

2

What Is It?

WHEN I WAS a senior in college, I competed in the Dartmouth Winter Carnival x-c race one cold morning in February 1950. After the race I had to hurry and hike back to my room, shower, and get ready for the afternoon's slalom event at Woodstock. As I was stepping out of the shower in the bathroom a bunch of us shared, two guys from next door were just getting up. They wandered in with their toothbrushes, saw me, took hold and remembered what was going on, and wished me good luck for the day's coming events. They didn't know I had already finished the x-c race. But then, they probably didn't know there was an x-c race at Carnival. That's the way it was then.

Several years later, during the late '60s, one of my housemates from that year at college wrote me a note and in effect said, "Hey Caldwell, how come you didn't tip us off to x-c in those days? We never realized what you were doing and how much fun it was. What a great sport!"

I never felt protective of x-c, trying to keep it to myself and a select group of friends. But there is always such a segment in any sport like this and sometimes they are the first to grumble when "their" sport becomes more popular, or changes.

Cross-country was bound to become more popular than it was in the late '40s and '50s and the changes are mind-boggling. Imagine listening to a morning weather report in Vermont and having the weatherman tell you that tonight is going to be one of the best nights of the year for moonlight x-c skiing. Better get out there, and if you can't ski, take a walk anyway and enjoy the light. Or, imagine

7

Start of the American Birkebeiner in Hayward, Wisconsin, the largest race on the North American continent.

Then there's the solitude of it all.

x-c ski areas investing in snowmaking equipment. Just a few years back, there were very few x-c areas and they were slow in gaining acceptance.

Now we are seeing more of the mass market approach to x-c. The parallels in the development of x-c with that of Alpine skiing are striking. After equipment went modern and changed from wood to fiberglass and other synthetics, the clothing became more stylized, waxes more specialized, and cosmetics on the equipment more hype. Area operators meet regularly now and discuss skier service; professional ski instructors have their rallies and other clinics, and why not? You can't find a sport with any degree of popularity that is not exposed to these changes, which are for the good of the most people. Even knowledgeable people in racing circles admit we need more skiers in order to become more competitive on the international circuit.

Telemarking I

There are some authors who try to lump in present-day Telemark skiing with cross-country skiing and I think that's a mistake. It may be that the x-c influence was the primary one in the recent rediscovery of Telemarking, but now Telemarking has enough variety and character to stand on its own feet.

A large percentage of today's Telemarkers ride ski lifts up hills. That clearly is not cross-country skiing. They use equipment that is becoming more and more like Alpine equipment and less and less like cross-country equipment. That's not cross-country skiing either. So, let's cut whatever cord that remains.

As for me, I like all forms of skiing. I'm presently enjoying a ski pass at a nearby Alpine resort and did more "Piney" skiing before Christmas 1986 than I had done in the three previous years. Loving it all, too.

There are so many facets to x-c and several people may have slightly different feelings about each, so I ask you:

What about Telemarking? I say that Telemarking is Telemarking, a part of skiing, but not part of cross-country skiing. There, I've said it! What do you think?

What about back-packing trips on x-c touring skis, or mountain skis? Is this x-c skiing, or camping, or both? What if you use snow-shoes instead of skis?

What about many books written in connection with x-c? Say, a book on x-c inns. Is this x-c or is it a study of inns and their offerings? How about an x-c cookbook? Is that x-c?

How about x-c tours abroad? Do these come under travel, or x-c?

There are always exercises you can do in your home, or the gym, for x-c skiing. X-C?

Back country touring.

I don't care so much about the answers to these questions, but feel pleased that so many good things are being associated with x-c skiing. For instance, the books probably provide vicarious pleasure for many people.

Since the sport enjoys such a wide range of applications, there are bound to be a few conflicts, or a bit of serious tongue waggling about certain features. Right now, some skiers can't accept trail fees charged by x-c ski areas. Most of these skiers are people who have been skiing free all their lives and suddenly find themselves in a position where they are being asked to pay. They might have been shut off from their favorite free skiing area, or they might have moved to a new job and can find only x-c-for-pay areas.

I wish all these grumblers could have a hand at cutting and maintaining ski trails during the offseason, and then take a few days at setting tracks on a snowmobile. I have never done such hard work in my life as setting tracks with an Alpine snowmobile. Most people simply can not manage this task in the rough terrain we have around here. We've burned out about 10 staff members at the Putney School, people who have taken one season on track-setting. They always go back to the director and offer to do anything but. . . .

WHAT IS IT?

Now, some x-c areas have bought powerful machines to do their grooming and this makes life easier for the drivers. But, when you get a new, big machine, you often find out that your trails are too narrow in many places, or that the bridges that used to hold your snowmobile will not stand up under the weight of that new monster. So, it's back to the summer trail maintenance, more expense, and wider trails. The investment for one of the smaller of the powerful machines brings the cost of grooming up to about $50 an hour, according to one figure. And you wonder why ski areas have to charge fees? You shouldn't. It's great to ski free in state and national parks, or in unbroken snow wherever you are lucky enough to find it, but please don't knock the ski areas that are trying to provide a different service for the public.

Many communities, schools, colleges, and clubs have x-c trails of their own, or trails on land that they have permission to use. Since the advances in the sport, many of these trails are outdated. They are too narrow and dangerous and need to be redesigned so they are safer and wider. Fiberglass skis and waxes make travel much faster now, and snow compaction adds one more element of speed to the equation.

Several smaller areas are faced with the problem of how to change their trails. If you have a trail that goes up a narrow, eastern gully, surrounded by ledge on both sides, there isn't a whole lot you can do to widen it. If you have a trail in the great expanse of the west, often all you have to do is pack it wider and you're OK. I tell you about these two extremes so you can be more knowledgeable and aware.

There's no doubt in my mind that the best place for most x-c skiers is an x-c ski area. Well-run areas have such a wide variety of services that it's a pity not to take advantage of them. And many of them need your support, having been through some hard winters. Check out their grooming, their trail systems, their teaching staff, ski shop, lunch room, rest room facilities, and the whole bit. It's a good place to meet people with similar interests. Season passes are never very much, either. I'll say more about areas in chapter eight.

Despite all these advances in the sport, there is still a nice lag between it and Alpine skiing. I love Alpine skiing and at the same time, I marvel at some of the obvious differences between the people and the areas that go with both types of skiing.

Some Alpine areas are getting the look and feel of jet airports, what with their parking garages and noises from the snow guns that are continually in operation. Skiers wheel up to unloading spots in vehicles of all sorts, just like airports, jump out and grab their equipment, and rush off to the ticket counter while someone else parks the car, or bus. Instead of lots of airport motels surrounding ski areas, we find more and more condominiums, some going for around half a million dollars. The prices for Alpine equipment still far outstrip those for x-c stuff, as do the tickets for skiing. But, in good snow years, the Alpine areas are booming anyway.

Then there's the lowkey x-c area where you can easily get stuck in the parking lot and the trail pass ticket seller may be out giving a lesson when you arrive. Brown-bag lunches adorn the tables and a smell of x-c wax replaces the smell of french fries at an Alpine base lodge. Sometimes goods are sold on the honor system because the staff is too small and busy to stand guard over the store. If you arrive in the middle of the morning, you may not find anyone in the x-c hut. They'll all be out skiing. There may even be just one toilet, or an outhouse, instead of all those toilets you find lined up side by side at an Alpine area. Pretty small potatoes, but pretty nice too.

It's not that all x-c areas are that lowkey. Many do exist and you can find them, and there are plenty that are more obviously out to please the customers. Which leads to my next point.

My pitch has always been that you make out of x-c exactly what you want. It's OK to swing along with the current fashions or trends if that's what you like. But if you want to keep using your wood skis, God bless you. Most x-c'ers are very tolerant and respect everyone's right to do what they want to do. It's an attitude you don't find in every sport and that is one of the wonderful features of x-c.

There is still the question about what this sport is. My friend Mike Brady says it's a sport with something for everyone, and that

WHAT IS IT?

may be the best definition there is. In general, there is just plain skiing. This can be a social occasion, or a solitary one. It can be done almost anywhere there is snow, but these days a large percentage of x-c skiing is done on prepared snow. At the other end of the scale, there is racing, but I'm only telling stories about that part of x-c.

There used to be a battle raging on semantics. One faction wanted x-c skiing to mean racing and ski-touring to mean x-c skiing—oops, I mean ski-touring to mean anything but racing, I guess. As I've said before, I've skied lots of courses with a bib on and in front of certain audiences, I say, "Oh yes, I raced in that one." With my buddies in the racing world, I have to admit that I was touring. But in any event, I feel that I was x-c skiing.

Now the differences may boil down to what one means by saying he is going skiing. Ski jumpers talk about skiing, meaning what I used to call ski-jumping. In some communities skiing means x-c skiing; in others, it means Alpine skiing. Our language really does not have enough different words or terms for all the situations we encounter in skiing, so we often have to qualify simple words like skiing.

The Female Connection

In my early days' involvement in x-c, there was no such thing as females skiing in this country. To be sure, a large number of women skied Alpine, but I'm afraid many people, females included, considered x-c as being too rugged for them. When I skied in school and college, it never occurred to me that women would ski x-c anymore than they would play on tackle football teams, I guess. So I never thought about the lack of female participation then.

When I wrote one of the early editions of this book, I mentioned the use of ski bags, which weren't a common item on the market. Naively, I suggested getting a mother or a girlfriend to sew one for the reader. Well, did I take heat for that one—from the women's libbers. That's OK. I deserved it. But I wish a few of those critics would turn around and acknowledge those who have worked hardest to get females into x-c skiing.

In the mid-'50s at Putney, we introduced the first junior relay race ever held in the states. Right now it does not seem like a significant event and perhaps it wasn't. But we thought it just natural that juniors should not be excluded from these fun races. Since Putney is a coeducational school, it seemed just as natural that girls should be allowed to race if they wanted. The problem was, there weren't any who skied x-c, or had the equipment. One girl student, however, named Martha Rockwell, wanted a crack at it. That year she borrowed some equipment and skied in the first leg of the Putney Relays. No one really knew there was a girl competing in this event because with all that baggy winter gear on, it was hard to differentiate between sexes. And no one even suspected a girl might be starting.

Martha took off and skied well in that race, beating in several boys. When a boy from Kimball Union Academy found out he had been beaten by a girl, he took his skis and smashed them against the hockey rink that was next to the starting area. Just shows you the feeling about girls' skiing that existed in those days.

As late as 1966, there was not much organized skiing for females in this country. Bob Tucker, the manager for our World Championship Team trip to Norway that year, and I met with the leader of the Swedish women's team, Inga Lowdin, after the meet and made arrangements for three of their skiers to visit the United States the next year. It was to be a PR mission for women's skiing and the trip turned out to be a tremendous success.

When the announcement was made about the Swedes' visit, everyone expected a bunch of Amazon-like females to show up. The Swedish Ski Association knew what it was doing and sent three very attractive women. They were Aase Karrlander, Toini Gustafsson, and Barbro Martinsson. Besides being attractive, they could ski fast and Toini and Barbro beat the pants off most of the men they raced against that season. Next year, at the Olympics, Toini won a couple of medals.

As you can imagine, the Swedes drew a lot of attention with their skiing feats and clinics. At one small reception we had for them in Putney, they talked Martha Rockwell into racing the next day, just

WHAT IS IT?

for the fun of it. This was the real start of Martha's career. She went on for several years before retiring from competition and turning to coaching. Most people agree she has been our best female skier to date.

In 1970 we sent our first women's team to a World Championships, in Czechoslovakia, and since then we have been regularly involved on the international circuit. More and more females have been racing, touring, and enjoying the sport. But the significant year for women's skiing in this country was 1967, when the Swedes visited the states.

So now, x-c *is* a sport for everybody. It's something people in the snowbelt can enjoy daily, with very little preparation or effort. For those less fortunately situated, there are increasing numbers of areas and some that have pretty fancy lodges associated with them too, I might add. You can travel to these just like the Alpine skiers do on their treks. Many Alpine areas have x-c adjuncts and these are often used as a break from Alpine skiing, or during inclement weather on the slopes. The sport is no longer a mystery, or a secret. It can be enjoyed by everyone in some way.

3

Equipment

EQUIPMENT is all that stuff that enables you to go skiing. It includes boots, poles, bindings, clothing, skis, and for many other people, lots of other items. The most important thing to remember about equipment is that it allows you to ski. If you're happy with what seems to be a minimum amount of equipment, don't let reading a lot of ads impress you too much.

My parents gave me some skis when we lived in Pennsylvania during the late '30s and I went out on them once. I'll never forget them . . . pine beauties with the little extra tip protruding from the real tip of the ski, and leather toe-straps.

I guess I had seen some pictures of people skiing and after we got a good snowfall, I hiked in my galoshes out to the nearest hill, pointed the skis down, and stepped into them. Few people knew about poles then, so I was without them and had to squeegie along to get going, but then, off I went plowing through the powder! I got about 20 yards, lost my balance, fell, and it felt good landing in that fluff. The only problem was that when I got up, one ski had gone to the foot of the hill. Undaunted, I traipsed down and hauled it back to my starting spot. Next time down I got considerably farther by following my tracks, but with the same result. One ski fell off and ended up at the bottom of the hill. From a safety aspect, I really didn't need runaway straps because there was no one else skiing, but straps might have prolonged my first day on skis. As it was, I got pretty tired and trudged home after a few runs. That was my skiing for the '30s. I had a ball. Little did I realize that anyone would need anything else in order to go skiing. Or that there was anything else to skiing except going downhill in a straight line.

I came to real skiing country in 1941 when my family moved to Putney, Vermont. In those days, virtually everyone at the Putney School, which I attended, skied and so the first winter here I got equipped with new leather boots, Dovre ski bindings, and Ski Sport Alpine skis. My father heard that one learned skiing best without poles and so I was without them for about two days. We got that straightened out.

This was the real beginning of my skiing career . . . wood skis, bamboo poles, and cable bindings with side hitches to allow those flexible leather boots to bend when climbing up hills or doing Telemark turns.

As you can imagine, the equipment we used then was quite versatile and closer to present-day Telemarking equipment than to today's standard Alpine equipment. Being so versatile we were able to practice all the latest Swiss, Austrian, and French turning techniques as well as those Telemark turns. For Telemark turns we simply unhitched the cables. We always practiced them in deep snow since they worked better than anything else in these conditions. I remember my first coach, John Holden, taking particular delight in teaching these turns. He was darned good at them, too.

When we skied up mountains or long trails, we used either skins or ski wax—like Sohm's Orange—to help us get up. I was amazed that a wax could help me to climb straight up a hill and then slide well going back down the slope.

It wasn't long before I began competing and it was then that I became exposed to all the science and folklore of equipment, waxing, training, and lots of other things.

We were going to the State High School Championships in 1946 and the team needed cross-country skiers in order to compete. My coach at that time, Rink Earle, asked me to volunteer to race x-c, even though I had no skis. I had to swipe my little sister Ruthie's five foot wooden downhill skis, complete with no edges, for the meet. My Alpine boots just barely fit in her bindings when they were extended to full width and when the race started, off I went, galloping around the course. I thought at the time the skis were quite a hindrance and I could have done better without them.

Somehow, our team did well enough at this meet to qualify for the New England High School Championships the next week-end. The team was pretty excited and so on our return to Putney, we thought we would train for the next cross-country race. We'd show 'em. So, we went out one day during that week, got pretty tired very quickly, and cashed in that idea.

But we went to the New Englands and I'll never forget the look of amazement on our faces when we moved into the local school gym to wax our skis. A lot of coaches were running around, frantically waving gasoline blowtorches at skis and racers, heating pine tar, changing waxes, questioning each other, and in general putting on quite a scene. We only had one wax—that Sohm's Orange—and had never heard of pine tar or any of that other stuff. We felt a little out of it in there, but if you think that was bad, you ought to have seen the results. We nailed down three or four of the last five places in the race and went home pretty subdued. I gave back my sister her skis and figured that was the end of my cross-country skiing, thank goodness!

I had done well enough in the Alpine events and ski-jumping at Putney to want to continue competitive skiing when I went to college at Dartmouth in 1946. Our head coach was Walter Prager and in about two sessions during my sophomore year, he got me so enthused about cross-country that I never gave it up. But I'm getting ahead of myself.

During my freshman year at college, we went to a local meet at Kimball Union Academy and the team needed cross-country skiers to fill in for the overall score and, guess what? I volunteered again. As usual, I had no equipment and so Walter lent me his. That was neat, as I might have said, but the only problem was that I couldn't keep the skis and bindings attached to his boots, which were on my feet at the time. I must have finished last. Once again I ended up feeling the skis were a hindrance.

Later in that season, the coaches sent me along to an x-c meet in Rumford, Maine. Probably had extra space in the cars. They knew I

EQUIPMENT

still had no equipment, but I was able to borrow stuff from the Nordic coach, Ja Densmore. This time the skis came off only when I fell after every downhill. Maybe Ja was better at putting on his bindings than Walter. Having learned from experience in Pennsylvania in the late '30s and during my first college race, I developed a clutching fall, grabbing hold of everything that was loose in the vicinity. So the skis never actually got away from me and I felt proud. I finished twenty-sixth in that one. Well, I may have been the last official finisher, but there were a lot of others who did not finish. (And I remember all your names, too!) I figured I was just about the twenty-sixth best skier around at that time.

That sums up my racing career through my first year in college. Four races! Two on my sister's little Alpine skis and two on my coaches' equipment. If these races taught me nothing else, they showed me the value of having my own skis and keeping them in good shape.

When I started coaching at the Putney School in the early '50s I quickly got onto the idea of having an interclass ski meet at the end of each ski season. I always scheduled these events as late as possible in order to draw out the winter term season (a boarding school, you know) and so the cross-country race was often run after one of those spring snowstorms. In those days we packed our trails by skiing them in and so the track or snow surface was usually moisture-laden but the snow underneath was insulated from the warm weather and still pretty dry. In short, it was a waxer's nightmare. Oh yes, we knew waxing by then. I had been to the Olympics in '52 and Swix wax was already five or six years old. I made it a point not to help anyone with the waxing. I was not only trying to be neutral, but I was trying to teach some of my skiers the difficulties of waxing by letting them do it themselves. I'm in education, you see.

On one particular race day, one of the strongest skiers on the team, a fellow named Jay Quay, iced up very badly during the competition. He tried the usual procedures of skiing across hemlock limbs or branches protruding from the snow, and all that, but nothing seemed to clear the bottoms. In desperation he took off his skis and swung them like a baseball bat against the nearest birch tree. The snow popped off, but so did his bindings. The screws couldn't withstand the blow and tumbled into the deep snow, lost until late spring—in case anyone was looking for them. We thought that was pretty hilarious and something that could only happen on the high school level with slightly experienced skiers.

About 20 years later, when fiberglass skis and the first Adidas bindings were both new, the lead-off racer for Sweden in the World Championship Relay Race kicked right out of his ski during the start. The binding, still attached to the boot, popped off the ski because it had not been mounted correctly. The new fiberglass skis were light by virtue of having air, foam, or something else without much substance, right there in the middle of the ski where the binding screws normally get their bite. The Swede ran around the stadium until he could find someone else with another ski with the new binding on, put it on, and skied off trying to catch the pack. Unfortunately, the other binding popped off just then. Back to his friend for that other ski, and off again—only to be disqualified later for changing two skis.

Two years later, at the Olympics, a Russian relay racer broke the boot on another one of the new boot-binding systems. That finished his team for the day.

So, don't feel bad if you have equipment problems now and then. But try to learn something about the proper care of your equipment, and then use that knowledge. It's a lot easier to manage fiberglass skis than the old wooden ones and you should consider yourself lucky in this respect. We had to work hard on those wood bottoms to keep them smooth, splinter free, flat, and covered with at least a thin layer of pine tar . . . all this before waxing them. The skis often warped and sooner or later lost their life, or spring. No, don't let anyone tell you the equipment was better in the "good ol' days."

Skis—What to Get

Tourskiers these days are faced with a dilemma of having two kinds of equipment to think about. It's the racer influence again. Most

EQUIPMENT

serious racers now have two separate sets of equipment . . . one for skiing in classical races and one for freestyle races.

I don't race much anymore, but I have three pair of skis, actually. One for skating and two for classical. The classical skis are different, one being softer than the other and useful in powder conditions. The other pair I use in klister conditions. I have so-called classical bindings on the classical skis, and boots to fit them. The skating skis have bindings suited for my skating boots and I have two different pole lengths. Unless you get a chance to ski as often as I do in quite varying conditions, you don't need all this stuff.

The equipment for classical races is as we have known it for many years. The skating equipment is different in these ways: skis are generally about 10 cm shorter and a bit stiffer; boots are stiffer, higher, and provide more support for skating; bindings are designed to accommodate the skating technique and provide better lateral support (which is in part due to the stiffer boots) than classical bindings; and poles are longer and stiffer. In addition, some new poles have canted handles, which theoretically allow for more power in the skating moves. They're the poles that don't fit in your car trunk anymore.

If you want to try skating, my recommendation to you is this: obtain some longer poles and using your regular classical skiing equipment, go out and see how you like this technique. If you are taken with it and don't want to buy a new pair of skis, try shaping the tips of your skis, or bobbing them. With a template, a hacksaw, and an appropriate file to finish it off, you can cut off some excess tip and make the old skis easier to manage during your skating maneuvers. If you get so proficient at skating that you feel the need for stiffer skis and boots, and different bindings, then I guess you will have to go ahead and purchase that new equipment. But save those remodeled skis for classical. The new, shorter tips won't bother you much unless you get into a lot of deep powder.

Some companies have already come out with skis they consider suitable for skating and classical skiing. Look into these. It may be possible to get a pair of them and two different boots—one stiff and

Cutdowns

When we were getting started in x-c skiing after WWII, we had to use anything we could get hold of. During the war a lot of skis had been made for the ski troops and in typical military fashion, there were warehouses full of leftover equipment if one knew where to look.

The company that made Flexible Flyer sleds before the war shifted its production to skis and got hold of a lot of hickory for this purpose. The skis they made were probably the most rugged wooden ones ever made. So, after the war we got hold of these for a few dollars a pair and trimmed off the metal edges and had instant x-c skis.

We weren't really into sidecut patterns then and so felt comfortable enough guiding that bandsaw just as close to the edges as we could without hitting them, and that was that. Since the skis had so much good wood in them, it didn't make too much difference where you sliced them—you just ran into more good wood.

If you took a pair of present-day Alpine skis and tried to trim them to x-c dimensions, you would get an awful shock. The guts of the ski might spill out and all you'd have left would be a top layer and a bottom layer, flapping about.

But, if you want to manicure some classical x-c skis and make them look like skating skis, it usually works because the tips don't have much guts to them. They are pretty much top and bottom layers glued together, therefore uniform through their widths. And since the optimum sidecut for a skating ski may not be agreed on for a long time, you are OK with the sidecut of that classical ski.

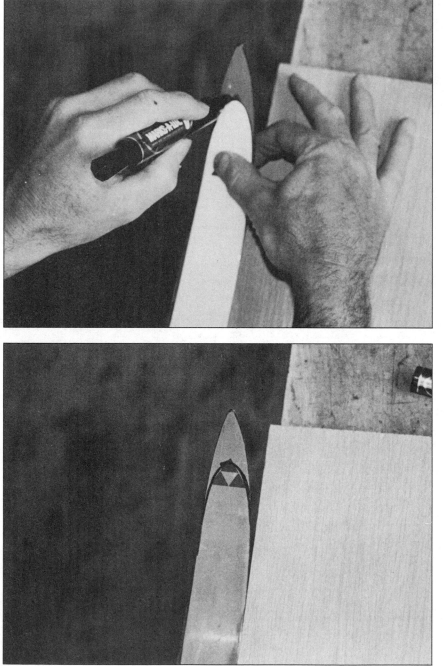

Shaping a classical ski tip for skating using a skating ski as a template.

Marked.

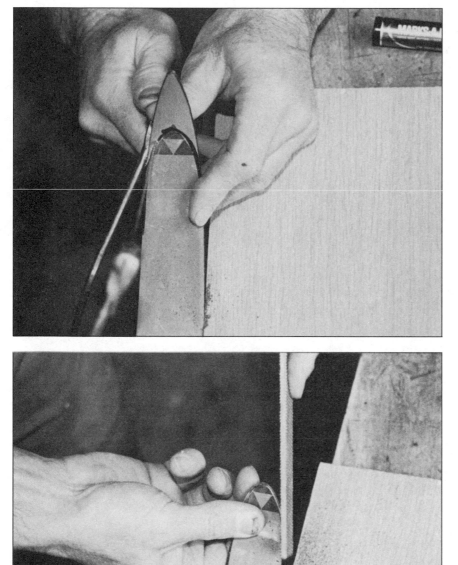

Trimming with a hacksaw.

Smoothing the tip.

EQUIPMENT

one more limber—and be in good shape. But, two pair of boots at this stage are not as necessary as two pair of poles. If you want to concentrate on classical skiing one day and skating another, you will definitely be better off with two lengths of poles. Sorry.

Naturally, the inclination for many skiers will be to use the same pair of skis for skating and classical. Not only that, they will probably try skating and classical during the same outing, but I can't recommend this. Any wax that is decent and works for classical will be nothing but a hindrance to skating. It will slow the skis and often will get worked out onto the sidewalls. When you try to skate and edge, with this stuff on the sidewalls, it will be doubly tough, and you may end up pulling some muscles in your upper leg or groin. Now, there *is* always the possibility that on one of your classical jaunts, your wax wears off, or slips badly. Well, you'll have to start skating!

If you decide to go pure classical, you can get waxable or waxless skis. Dealer's choice. But if you lean toward classic and think you may want to try skating with the same skis, you will have a hard time with most waxless skis since the drag on them will make it difficult. So, you get waxable skis as your only pair. Otherwise, if you want to skate and want waxless skis as well, it will have to be two pair of skis.

It's hard for me to imagine a tourskier opting for all skating, but there may be a few skiers who do. Get skating equipment and go for it. I hope you can find the proper conditions for skating every time you go out. If the snow is not well-packed everywhere you ski, it will be rough going.

Ski Flex

With luck, you can get a ski with the proper flex. Proper flex is something a lot of us talk about but find it hard to do much about. I guess I've had two or three pair of skis during my career that really had the right flex for me; that is, they wore evenly, the wax worked the way it was supposed to on tips, tails, and under the foot, and the skis seemed to glide along pretty well. Maybe I've been fussier, or unlucky. (Or, maybe my weight has varied too much from time to time, thus changing the way the skis work.)

You ought to be able to get something that is in the ballpark if you look over enough skis and get good advice. You need a ski that's going to work for your particular technique. Right now, with skating being so new and not requiring so many different waxes or a kick pocket under the foot, it's probably easier to get skating skis that will work reasonably well. For classical skiing you have to be sure the section under the foot, whether it's a waxless or a waxable ski, will make good contact with the snow when your weight is on the ski; otherwise, you won't have any grip and will have to start skating, or doing the herring-bone in order to get places.

A pretty good, old test for proper ski flex is as follows: stand on both skis on an even, hard surface and ask someone—perhaps the salesman—to see if a slip of paper will just barely slide out from under the wax pocket. If the paper sticks, the skis are too soft. If the paper slides in and out so easily that perhaps a piece of cardboard would do as well, given the space between the floor and the skis, your skis are too stiff. You'll have a hard time setting the wax, or the waxless section of the ski.

I'm not going to talk about torsional rigidity, forebody flex, or any of that stuff. If you're like me, those terms leave you cold. I just want something that works well for me and I know I have to try different skis in order to succeed. There are just too many variables that affect how my skis work under me, my own state of conditioning not being the least among them!

Boot-Binding Combos

There are quite a few boot-binding combinations, or systems, on the market. Salomon broke through with the first good one, which provided more support than any of us had been used to. Now, there are many other systems and again, your shop is key here. If they tout one system, and are familiar with it, you'll be best off going with them.

Be sure the system you get is the one appropriate for your technique, that is, classical or skating.

If you're considering altering some of your equipment to make another technique easier, like going from classical to skating, leave the binding placement the same. Early on, the skaters figured they would have better control over their ski tips if their bindings were mounted a few centimeters ahead of the balance point, so they moved them. Then their skis did not ride well because too much weight was concentrated on the front part of the ski, so back the bindings came. At about the same time, they settled for bobbing their tips, as described above.

Poles

With poles you generally get what you pay for. The market is quite competitive. For skating length poles, one company has recommended this formula: multiply your height in inches by 2.29 and that will give you your pole length in centimeters. I would go shorter rather than longer with this measurement. For classical skiing the old system of having the poles fit comfortably under your armpit works well. But if you are going to be into skating, you may eventually find you want a slightly longer pole for classical, since you will get used to a much longer skating pole.

Where to Get It—The Kit

After wading through this material, you may want to toss it in and go to a ski shop and order their special, which is usually considerably less expensive than buying the units separately. It's not a bad idea. It's easy to get confused, or read conflicting reports in lots of ads, especially when the companies began to take swipes at their competitors' products.

Even without getting the kit, the best place to go is a ski shop that specializes in x-c equipment. They should be up on the latest stuff and can give you recommendations on their products. The market is changing rapidly and items we take for granted now may be outdated in a matter of months.

Clothing

We used to ski in anything we could get hold of. After World War II, ski pants came on the market and they worked well for Alpine skiing and the ski-jumping that I did. But I was always puzzled as to what to wear for x-c and often ended up in khakis. Then knickers came along and we all talked about their advantages. The lower legs could pass each other in the diagonal stride without that brushing sound of pant leg on pant leg. Beside that, they looked good in that they marked us as x-c'ers.

In 1952 the Olympic Committee provided us with gray, nylon suits for racing. They were baggy by today's standard, but flashy for those days. Some of us noticed that our perspiration clung to our bodies and we got pretty cold on some days when we went down long hills after being in a full sweat. But we didn't know about polypropylene and all those goodies then.

For a long time, the tourskiers were ahead of the racers in the clothing department because they would cruise along in their woolies, stay warm even though they perspired, or got wet from snow or rain, and not suffer. I had a good pair of wool knickers and skied Alpine with them for many years in the '50s. I even raced downhill with them. But I didn't dare race x-c with them. You just didn't race in wool.

In 1972, our Olympic X-C Team broke in with the first racing suits. We still used knicker socks, but the suit was much tighter and faster than anything on the market at the time. It was about one year later that the Europeans came out with the first full length racing suit, about skin tight and very sleek.

These suits required warm-ups, for warming-up, obviously, and good underwear, and so the clothing manufacturers began to unravel the yet-to-end parade of outer garments and under garments. They are getting better all the time. Now the underwear wicks out perspiration and you can actually sweat without having a cold,

EQUIPMENT

clammy layer of clothing next to your skin, giving you windchill fits on downhill sections.

The advances made in clothing are almost as significant as the ones in hard equipment. Clothing is lighter, warmer, more functional, more colorful, less expensive, and can be used for a variety of other activities such as hiking, biking, running, Alpine skiing, and so on. In most weather, you can get along famously with some of that polypropylene underwear, or an equivalent, and a suit that can be either loose or one of those tight fitting jobs.

Accessories

I usually wear gloves when x-c'ing but if you are apt to get cold hands, you should go the mitten route. My favorites are still the so-called French Canadian racing gloves, those brown cotton work gloves I can buy at the Galanes' Sport Shop for $1.99. Some people swear by silk glove liners, whether they use gloves or mittens over them.

Goggles used to be more trouble than they were worth since they fogged up and you couldn't see where you were going. Now there are some good screens or shields that can protect you against wind, sun, and especially snow. It's no fun skiing at speeds on downhills during a snowstorm without protection for the eyes.

The deep powder skiers are usually equipped with gaiters to keep their lower legs from getting cold and wet. These aren't a bad thing for cold weather skiing on packed snow, either.

Wool hats are a must with me, but I am continually amazed at seeing people skiing with no hats, no earbands, and sometimes not much hair to cover up that head. When they go to an earband, I usually have two hats on. You can lose a lot of heat through your head, so keep it warm, especially on cold days.

Cold Weather Skiing

I used to think most skiers could generate enough heat to keep warm on the coldest days, but now I know better. I can't anymore and there must be a lot of you others in the same boat.

THE NEW CROSS-COUNTRY SKI BOOK

When it's cold I take all sorts of precautions, beginning with the feet. I have some store-bought'n boot-gloves, but they aren't always handy and then I just pull on an old athletic sock—one with a hole in the toe, either cut out by me, or one worn out by me—right over each ski boot. If I have a choice in boots, I take the warmest ones, but I don't pack on the socks because if my feet are too tight in there, they get cold, no matter what. I might go with an extra inner sole if it is not too tight-fitting.

Regular underwear, long underwear, ski suit, and warm-up pants adorn my lower half. I pull my long underwear on over my socks and that seems to keep my socks from sliding down and my underwear legs from sliding up toward my knee. I use full-sleeved top underwear, the kind that wicks perspiration, then put on a turtle neck under my suit if it's really cold. Otherwise I go with only a warm-up jacket over my suit. I use my Alpine gloves if it's necessary. One hat and an earband, or two hats top it off, along with a windscreen for my eyes and forehead. You'd be pleasantly surprised by how much heat you can conserve by wearing one of these things.

If I get cold wearing all these clothes, I know that I am tired. And I quit. Funny thing, when you're tired no amount of clothing can keep you warm. I didn't learn this until I had been skiing a long time. Had I known this earlier, when I was training more, I would have used this cold feeling as a training indicator and taken more time off. There is no good reason for suffering in the cold and you will be doing yourself a favor if you call it a day under these circumstances.

Equipment Care Pointers

If you get new skis and want to work on them yourself, you can make it simple, or about as difficult as you like.

I usually check to see if the bottoms are flat by drawing a square metal scraper along the surface. I check the squareness of the scraper against my T-square first. If the bottoms are not flat, I scrape them until they are. Scrapers occasionally need sharpening and I use a file for that, checking for squareness after each filing.

After scraping, I sand the bottoms smooth with fine sandpaper. Then I melt in some glide wax that is appropriate for the temperatures I'll be skiing in. If I'm going to ski classical and use kick wax, I leave the section under the foot free of glide wax since I'll put the other wax there. For skating, I iron the whole bottom with glide wax. After waxing, I scrape again, but this time with a plastic scraper, just so I don't take all the wax off, or score the bottoms in my haste.

I keep my ski bottoms waxed, whether I'm skiing classical or skating. They just work better and last longer. If you get skis with the new sintered bottoms, you are under more pressure to keep them waxed since they will tend to soak up water and impurities otherwise. I'll say more about waxing and rilling, or structuring, in the chapter on waxing.

Never jam your ski bottoms in the snow to stand them up while you take a break. This is one of the best ways to delaminate the tails.

Look for signs of delamination regularly. If you see something that looks suspicious, take it to the shop where you bought the skis, or take it to a shop that specializes in x-c repair.

Check your binding screws to make sure they are tight. Loose screws aggravate a bad situation and eventually you may end up without your boot and binding attached to the ski . . . like the Swede or the Russian mentioned above. Often the screws are put in with epoxy glue and adding a little more may solve the problem of loose screws. Some people still like to add match sticks and steel wool to the screw hole before glueing in that loose screw.

If you should have to remove your bindings and can't get the screws started, try heating them. If you have a blowtorch with a small burning tip, you can concentrate the flame on the screw head and not scorch the surroundings.

Keep your bindings and boot bottoms waxed or covered with something like silicon spray so as to cut down on snow build-up. Nothing is more frustrating than trying to fit your boot into a binding when the grooves and small spaces are filled with a mixture of snow, sand, and gravel.

Even with silicon your boot soles and bindings are apt to get plugged with some kind of junk. After each outing I bring my boots inside and run water from the faucet over the soles. This cleans them nicely. That's one advantage the synthetic soles have over the leather ones. You wouldn't want to make the leather soles any wetter and so therefore wouldn't expose them to water in the sink. I also try to knock out the stuff stuck in and around the binding and if this fails, I bring the skis inside to warm and hope it will melt away.

Check your pole baskets to make sure they are not loose, or wearing out, or rotating. Many are glued with epoxy, and running very hot water over them will allow you to twist the baskets, or take them off completely. Realign them, after adding a bit of epoxy, and let it harden.

Try and protect your pole shafts since a lot of them suffer badly from cuts, or slices. They are apt to break under these conditions, much the same way as a pane of glass does when you score it and then give it that little tunk to break it in two.

Keep your boots in good shape. Ask your dealer what should be done here.

Check the fit between your boot and binding, at least once a year. Many times, after extensive use, bindings and boots wear out and there is a lot more play between them than there was when they were new. Control becomes more difficult in this situation. There isn't too much you can do here except get new equipment, saving the old stuff for gentle skiing.

Look at your pole straps to make sure they are not cut or wearing thin in some places. A bit of adhesive tape wrapped around these weak parts will prolong strap life.

A Short Summary

Here are the major considerations when making purchases.

Skis: for classical, follow the usual recommendations. Get skis whose tips you can cup your hand over comfortably and try to get a good flex. If you're skiing in a lot of tracks, you will be happy with the narrow skis; otherwise, get a wider, touring width. For skating, get the specialized skating model. It will be shorter and stiffer.

For both styles of skiing, get a combination ski, using the advice of your shop's experts.

Boot-binding combinations: with the introduction of combination skis, you will surely have a choice of boot-binding combinations that will do nicely. This is probably the way to go unless you feel certain you will be doing all classical, or all skating.

Poles: for skiing the two styles, you are going to need two pair of poles. Get the classical ones a bit longer than usual because you will soon get used to them. The skating poles ought to reach close to the height of your chin.

T-shirt skiing in Australia.

4

Technique — Classical

I HAD BEEN skiing Alpine for several years before I got seriously interested in cross-country. When we practiced slalom in those days, we usually had to climb up the slope for each run through the gates. You can imagine we knew how to do the herring-bone and how to traverse across and up the slope, using the diagonal technique. At some of the important downhill races on the mountain trails, many of us used skins wrapped around our skis for uphill traction to get to the top. This was always the most gruelling part of the day, getting to the top with enough energy left to race back down. If the coach was not along, we had to wrap the skins around our waist and race with them flapping in the breeze—hardly the picture of aerodynamics. But in using skins, we all got an idea of what it was like to climb straight up a hill and of course we had to use our arms in the same way x-c skiers do today when climbing hills. As I have mentioned earlier, it was possible to do all this climbing because we had cable bindings with low hitches and high hitches and all we had to do was loosen them for our climbs. The boots were just a little stiffer than today's Peter Limmer climbing boots.

With this background in Alpine skiing, it was a fairly easy transition to learn x-c. However, in college I was not very sophisticated in my use of x-c technique. It was pretty much straightforward and as fast as I could manage. The double-pole was pretty popular when the track conditions allowed but most of the time, we were doing a fast shuffle without much glide.

I went to the Olympics in 1952 as a Nordic-combined skier along with three other teammates. We were the top of the heap here in the

States but had never been exposed to the Europeans, and Scandinavians in particular. Our best skier was Ted Farwell and I'll never forget his report of the 18 km race. He was whistling along up a hill, doing a pretty fast herring-bone, and the top Finn, Heikki Hasu, caught him right there. The trail was narrow and would not allow two skiers doing the herring-bone to pass. That was no problem for Heikki because he was skiing straight up the hill anyway. He stepped right on the front part of Ted's ski—good grip there, I guess—as he went by and disappeared over the top of the hill.

I wasn't good enough to make our relay team at the '52 Olympics and our top skiers, mostly special x-c racers, did their best in the morning relay race a few days later. That afternoon the ladies used the same course for their special 10 km race and a bunch of women from the Finnish team had times that were faster than our men's best in the relay.

You can see that we were a bit behind in certain phases.

Undaunted, most of us stayed with the sport. I began coaching and in 1954 or 1955, Bob Pidacks, a member of the '52 x-c team and the '54 FIS Team, came back from Europe to help with a junior training camp I was working at. He took me out one afternoon and showed me the one-step double-pole and it was a real revelation. Before this, we had always used at least two steps to get into a double-pole. I've alluded to our lack of conditioning compared to world class skiers but the main reason for this two-step double-pole was the old-fashioned equipment, which was heavier and slower than today's, and the tracks, or lack of tracks. We were often pushing snow with our ski tips and under these conditions it's hard to get up a head of steam.

In fact, two of my buddies in Colorado, Sven Wiik and Dolph Kuss, were studying technique at the same time and giving names to various maneuvers. They came out with this thing called three steps and more. It was just another way to lead into a double-pole and when I thought about all the powder snow those poor guys had to push around, I realized the need for such a technique. I mean, if you are wallowing in snow halfway to your knees, you'd need at least

THE NEW
CROSS-COUNTRY
SKI BOOK

three steps and probably a slight downhill slope to get enough speed to make a double-pole worthwhile.

In 1957 Rick Eliot came back from a year's study in Norway with a movie solely devoted to technique. This was a major breakthrough and stood a lot of coaches on their ears because it challenged them to think about things. To look at the film today, you would think most of the notions were outrageous, but they were hot stuff in those days. I always thought Rick's film did more to get us studying technique than anything before, or since. He broke down the various elements of technique and introduced some new things like side-bending (which has since gone out). But here was a film, dedicated solely to x-c! What a big deal!

So, because of a lack of exposure to the better x-c skiers, and because we were not well-advanced in course preparation, we certainly lagged behind the rest of the world in skiing techniques for a long time. This was true for the tourskiers as well, what few there were then. I got my tipoff when we were in Norway before the Olympics in 1952 and some of us were staying with a local banker. He offered to take us on a tour one day, out to one of the huts for lunch, and then back. He was one of those week-end skiers, a tourskier, really, and we thought this would be a piece of cake. But he skied us right into the ground. When Tom Jacobs and I got back to our room that night, we compared notes and said, "If this guy doesn't ski that much, and the Norwegians on the team actually train a lot, what are we in for?" Exactly.

Progress

Few sports exist that have not witnessed major technique changes during the past 30 to 40 years, but the changes in skiing techniques have been more significant than changes in any other sport I know of. The new skating techniques have really topped them all.

There are several reasons for these changes and I'll cite the most important ones.

TECHNIQUE —
CLASSICAL

Vintage photo. U.S. Team practicing synchronization drills at Rabbit Ears Pass, Colorado, in the late '60s.

Competition has increased and when countries begin vying for honors at Olympic Games and World Championships, they research everything that will help them. Skiers train more, gain strength and abilities to perform better, and these changes eventually—rather quickly, in fact—get passed on to the tourskier.

Ski equipment has been keeping pace with individual physical improvements. No one could have dreamed of going so fast, or skating, with the equipment we used in the '40s and '50s. Waxes are better and faster. Skis are more rugged yet lighter, better designed, and faster. All the other equipment is much lighter too. All this conspires to make much more possible in the way of new, faster techniques.

Finally, snow grooming has helped make possible all these new techniques. Compare the old days when we skied out our tracks and were lucky indeed if there was a pole track at all. Now, the snow can be packed so it is smooth and firm. Tracksetters make track skiing a delight. They were bound to come because so many skiers worked so hard to prepare courses for races that someone had to think of a better way.

At the 1960 Olympics in Squaw Valley, the course workers got up about 3 A.M. on every race day, ate breakfast, donned their headlamps and ski equipment, and headed out to ski in the tracks for the races, some of which began at 7:30 A.M. Tough duty for a bunch of volunteers.

At the 1966 FIS in Oslo, they had a big snowstorm the night before the 50 km race and had to call in all the army reserves to prepare the trail. They shovelled the snow off in many sections since that was more effective than trying to pack it with skis. The course was fairly firm under the new snow so this idea made good sense. The only problem was that the track was over 15 miles long! Tough duty for a bunch of soldiers too, but they had to do it.

I'm going to lay claim to being with the first club to use snow machines for packing snow. The Putney School was given a Ski-Doo in 1964 and we immediately began using it to pack our trails. That worked so well that Bob Gray, who was working with me, designed what I'll also claim as one of the first tracksleds, if not the first. It was

Homemade tracksled, pictured after several seasons of use.

TECHNIQUE—
CLASSICAL

just a couple of claws tacked onto a wood frame weighted down by a cement block, all of which we dragged behind the machine. But what a pleasure it was to ski in pre-set grooves—I won't call them tracks, really, since we still had to ski them in, but they were evenly spaced, and faster than anything we had encountered before.

Finally, in 1968, at the Olympics in France, the organizers got the idea of using a big snow-packing machine with a tracksled dragged behind. This was a huge jump forward because the sled set double tracks. From this time up to and including the present, track-setting and snow preparation devices have been getting more and more sophisticated. We all can benefit from these advances.

But don't be too quick to accept everything that comes along. At the 1972 Olympics in Sapporo, the Japanese did a very conscientious job. They had already been to the '68 Games to make notes and did those tracksleds one better. The only problem was that they had some squirrely downhill sections on their courses and did not lift the tracksled from the snow on any of the corners. The result was that skiers following the tracks would get flipped right out of them because they were curved and the skis were straight, so something had to give. I'll never forget my first experience there. Having struggled to the top of a hill, I was in a resting tuck with my head down, gaining speed and suddenly, I was thrown right to the outside of the track and down over a bank into a pile of deep snow. If someone hadn't seen me and helped me out, I might still be there.

Techniques

Until the early '80s, there was one basic technique, the diagonal, or single stride, now called classical. Everyone used it, many books and many chapters in many books have been written about it, and it's still around. But typically, the racers caught onto something that was faster and started skating.

Now, the ski world is split between the two techniques, and while there are many similarities between the two, it doesn't follow that if you can do one, or learn one, you will have an easy time with the other technique.

Meanwhile, the governing body of international ski competition, the FIS, has determined that half of the big races during the next few years will be classical and half will be freestyle, meaning anything, including skating, is allowed. Skating will be allowed on certain sections of classical races, such as corners, but the details really don't concern us now. What is important is that classical skiing has been given a reprieve and chances are pretty good that we will have two major types of events during every season, classical and freestyle. It may mean an increased number of events at the Olympic Games, but the overall effect on tourskiers will be to keep classical skiing. I think that's good. There's something about classical technique that any practiced skier enjoys. As for me, classical is a lot easier on my overused joints.

To further the life of classical skiing, a group of people from several countries have formed the World Classic Grand Prix, a series of eight marathon races in which only the classical technique is allowed. If this series survives, it will be interesting to compare its fields with most of the Worldloppet Series, where freestyle skiing is the rule.

If you ski in a lot of unbroken snow, classical is for you. Don't try skating too often unless you want to feel frustrated.

If you want to skate, you had better be sure that you have some terrain that is well-packed and wide enough, otherwise you will come a cropper. On the other hand, if you are a classical skier, you can always get along without tracks and can use the snow that is prepared for skating. You may get some strange looks when the skaters go by you, but if you are worried about little things like this, perhaps you shouldn't be skiing x-c in the first place.

As I mentioned earlier, skating appears to be much harder on some of the joints—like knees and hips—than classical skiing. My hunch is that older skiers will end up preferring the classical technique.

Some Norwegian doctors came out with a paper, soon after the advent of skating, warning skiers of dire effects on the joints from prolonged skating maneuvers. Skating is still young and I think it's too early to know about such things as occupational hazards. But, I

TECHNIQUE—
CLASSICAL

side with the doctors for another, perhaps God-given reason. If we had been destined to skate on skis, I think many of our joints would have been redesigned before birth. There isn't much doubt in my mind that classical skiing is a more natural motion for our body and our joints. I've said it's more natural than walking, so you can see where I stand.

Importance of Technique

I have always felt that technique was the most underrated part of skiing. Countless people spend hours on waxing, training, equipment, mindsets, and things like that, but I spend hours on technique—maybe because I enjoy studying it so much. The rewards of practicing and improving one's technique are so great. It just feels better when you ski and you're more efficient, meaning you can ski farther and longer and enjoy it just that much more.

Despite my love for technique, it took me many, many years to learn a good way to teach it well. Now I have it and it's called doing drills. I was brought up to abhor drills and I can't really explain why. But I figured therefore no one else would enjoy doing drills and I did not use them extensively for the first 20–25 years of my coaching career. We used to practice techniques—no doubt about that—but we didn't really drill!

I was forced into using drills one year at Putney when about 30 kids came out for the team. I didn't know how to handle this large group because the abilities varied so much. I had used the old method of having the better skiers teach the beginners, and all that, but it was always hard for me to control the sessions the way I wanted.

I thought I would thin out the crowd of 30 by putting them through a whole bunch of drills—like double-poling across this field five times, with no strides. Then doing it another five times with one stride for each double-pole. And so on. I'd soon see who was serious about this sport! The first workout, and subsequent ones, averaged to about 45 minutes—back and forth, back and forth. After drills, being the nice guy that I am, I would let them go skiing on the trails.

Well, the kids came out and did the drills and for a couple of days, no one quit the team. After about four days of drills, some other kids started coming up to me to ask if it was too late to sign up for the ski team, that they had heard it was so much fun! I was dumbfounded, but took them on because by then I realized how relatively easy it was to handle a large group with this system. And I could begin to see improvement in the skiers. So, I've stuck with this system.

I'm often asked about the effects of imagery training in learning to ski. I know it works fairly well for some people but I have a problem believing that everyone can see himself, or see another skier whose technique he might want to copy. I'm continually amazed at the responses I get from skiers when I ask them for comments on some of their colleagues' techniques. People see so many different, varied, and often wrong things that I wonder if they would be able to see the correct moves with their imagery.

But more important, I'm a firm believer in the marvelous capacity the body has to learn, adjust where necessary, and come out with some efficient movements for a given task, like skiing. It's usually a mistake to try and model your style after some world class skier such as Gunde Svan, because he has different muscles, different levers, different training, and so on. A certain body movement will work for him when it is well-nigh impossible for you to execute. But if you keep practicing and doing drills, your own body will begin to make adjustments as it gains in strength and coordination, and you will probably be skiing as efficiently as you can be. What else can one ask?

So I'm going to pass on to you some of my favorite drills for classical skiing. Practice them if you feel like it. I promise I won't check your reps.

Drills for Classical Skiing

You need tracks or well-packed snow for most of these drills, otherwise you'll have a hard time of it. In addition, your skis need to be waxed properly or your waxless skis should be as effective as well-waxed ones. I'm assuming you already have some experience

TECHNIQUE—
CLASSICAL

skiing. These drills will help you to improve. After this I will list four drills for beginning skiers.

❄ 1. Ski in tracks without poles. This is an old favorite and helps to develop good balance. It happens to be a good way to test your wax. If you can't ski up even the slightest incline, the chances are good you need more wax, or a different waxless ski bottom.

Skiing with no poles. Relaxed, too.

❄ 2. Ski around a small figure-eight course without poles. Be sure the loop you ski doesn't get you going so fast that you have to make a lot of step turns in order to stay in the track. This defeats the purpose of the drill, which is to learn to steer or guide your skis around those slight corners. It takes delicate lower leg and ankle control to keep your momentum in this one, especially when you do it without poles.

❄ 3. Ski the figure-eight course with poles. Now it will be easier and by using your poles, you will go faster. So the challenge becomes trying to eliminate the step turns again. There's nothing wrong with step turns, it's just that if you want to practice them, you practice them, and not this drill, which emphasizes a different technique.

❄ 4. Practice the scooter without poles in a straight track. In this one you kick, or push off one ski only. It's like pedaling or pumping along on a scooter. This drill develops the knack of setting the wax on one ski. Naturally, you have to alternate skis so you can do it off both equally well. I usually practice kicking most off my weaker leg.

❄ 5. Double-pole, with no kicks or strides, for long stretches of track. This one helps to develop your technique and your strength. When it gets easy, pole up slight hills, then steeper ones.

Double-poling with no steps. Getting ready to plant the poles.

TECHNIQUE —
CLASSICAL

The push. Notice the hands are below the head and shoulders.

The follow-through.

Recovery. Getting ready to plant the poles again.

THE NEW
CROSS-COUNTRY
SKI BOOK

After you plant your poles, get your hands below your shoulders so your upper body weight can provide most of the force as you lean over and down in the poling motion.

❆ 6. Single-pole along the track with no strides. Just sheer arm power. It's OK to bob with the upper body in this one. You'll find it helps to get a rhythm by leaning forward onto each pole. The poling motion should extend well beyond the hip, so far in fact, that a person standing off to the side can see daylight between your rear arm and hip.

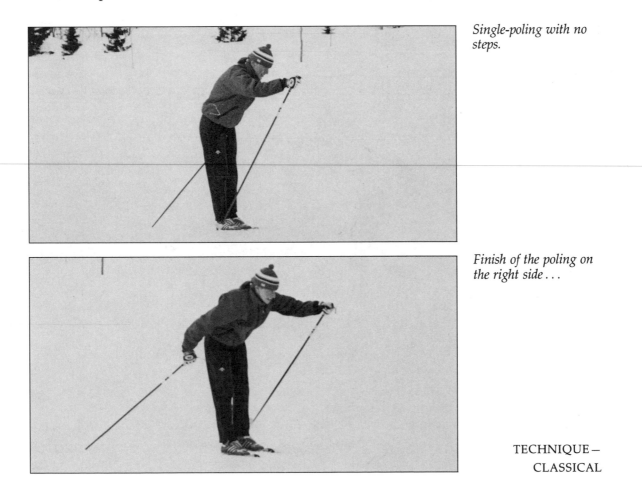

Single-poling with no steps.

Finish of the poling on the right side . . .

TECHNIQUE —
CLASSICAL

. . . as right arm swings forward and pole is planted.

It's natural for the body to sit back a bit in this drill.

❄ **7.** Double-pole with one stride, or kick. Once again, be sure you can kick off either leg. Or, concentrate kicking off your weaker leg.

Double-poling with one step. Poles being planted with weight on left ski, getting ready to kick off it.

Follow-through.

Reaching forward to plant again.

TECHNIQUE—
CLASSICAL

❄ **8.** Same as 7, but alternate kicking legs. Done properly, this one develops a nice rhythm.

❄ **9.** Practice the diagonal (or classical, or single step) on a slight downhill track to see how far you can extend your stride. Don't worry about exactly coordinating your arm and leg movements as you would when skiing along the flat, but just soar out over the forward ski as far as you can without tipping over, and see how long you can hold it before switching to the other ski. The balance and strength you build doing this will also have a good effect on your skating technique.

❄ **10.** Practice the herring-bone, up a hill obviously. After you get comfortable with this step, experiment by taking shorter, quicker steps. Try getting more bite with the edge of your ski, and even the binding, by bending the ankles in more. See how much you can

Two good herring-bones.

THE NEW
CROSS-COUNTRY
SKI BOOK

change the angle your skis make with the direction of the track, or uphill. The smaller the angle, the better, in general . . . until you start to slip.

Check the position of your hips. If you are bent too much at the waist, it's likely your hips are too far back and you will be moving too much weight up and forward with each step. Straighten up and bring the hips forward more. It works.

I would spend a lot of time doing the herring-bone, not because it is so much fun, but because it will tune up the skating muscles.

❄ **11.** Practice skiing downhill in tracks until you find a nice comfortable position you can hold at reasonable speeds. With good tracks your weight should be evenly distributed on the skis, your upper body and especially the arms, relaxed, and there should be a slight flex in the knees and ankles. My favorite position in good tracks is to bend over at the waist and rest my forearms on my legs, just above the knees. My hands are slightly crossed with poles out to the side. It's a bit faster than standing up because you present less of your body to the air resistance. You can check this by standing straight up and coasting out on a flat, then repeating the run with the slightly crouched stance I suggest. You should coast farther.

Crouching for just that extra bit of speed.

TECHNIQUE—
CLASSICAL

❄ **12.** On a smooth downhill surface, practice the straight snowplow until you can control your speed.

The snowplow.

❄ **13.** After you become proficient with the snowplow, try snowplow turns by simply weighting one ski more than the other. You will turn. Be sure to get it going both directions. This is one drill where it's not easy to practice to that weak side alone. How many right turns can you make without throwing in a left turn now and then?

❄ **14.** Move right on to stem turns, done by stemming (or snowplowing) one ski only. Weight it and go around.

This turn should be practiced at increasingly higher speeds until you have great confidence in it. Lots of skiers get into trouble and fall because they do not hold the stem through long, fast turns. It may not look fancy, or delicate, and it may not be as fast as skating or stepping around a turn, but it's a pretty sure bet. Just get the weight on the outside ski—outside in terms of the direction of the turn—and hold it right there. Persist!

❄ **15.** After you have mastered the snowplow and stem turns, you are ready to begin working on connected turns, or easy slalom courses. This adds an element of fun and practicality. Sneak into a group that is running easy gates and see what happens.

❄ **16.** Step turns, or skating turns, are best begun on the flats. Get the arms coordinated with your steps, or skates, before you move to downhill terrain. If your want to build more coordination and strength, set up some poles to skate around on a slight uphill. This is much better than moving to downhill sections to practice these maneuvers since you can get along without your poles on the downhills. On the uphills you need more strength and coordination, and that's good practice for you.

A step turn being executed to the left.

❄ **17.** If you can find an easy slope covered with new, unpacked powder snow, get right out there and try your turns, or methods for changing direction. You may be successful, depending on your

TECHNIQUE—
CLASSICAL

strength and the depth of the snow. If you are having troubles, it's a perfect time to begin practicing Telemarks. Slide one ski ahead so that your boot on this ski is right alongside the other ski tip. Then stem that forward ski slightly and see if you don't turn.

I don't want to get into big arguments about Telemarks. There are many different techniques for Telemarking. The method I describe is the one I learned, and when executed while maintaining a fairly upright position is the most graceful and difficult one. That's why I like it. It takes a time to get into the turn and it can be suspenseful, but when you go around, it feels great.

Kerrin Petty and Chris Clark doing synchronized Telemarks.

Oops!

TECHNIQUE –
CLASSICAL

An easier method, and the one I see executed most often on packed Alpine slopes, is done by dropping one ski back and getting in a fairly low crouch. This one is quicker and steadier because as you drop one ski, you immediately shift more weight to the other ski and stem or edge it. You go around quickly. But it's only a three or four in degree of difficulty.

Telemarking II

Around a hundred years ago, some Norwegians living in the Telemark Province invented some bindings that were an improvement over the toe-strap. They were able to steer their skis with these toe bindings and soon the Telemark turn came into being. It was definitely a deep snow turn because slopes and trails just weren't packed in those days.

For years the Telemark turn held forth on the cross-country scene—which amounted to just about all of skiing—until a major change took place in the 1930s. Then, along with the invention of ski lifts and Alpine skiing, it became clear that a skier could gain better control over his motions if the heels were held down. A loose heel wasn't needed for those rides on the lifts up the hill either. Leather thongs acting as cables were the first improvement, followed by metal cables. Sharp edges became necessary for better control on the Alpine slopes and metal edges were put on those wooden skis. Wider skis, stiffer skis, and skis with sidecut all followed. Stiffer Alpine boots and more elaborate bindings followed and we are still faced with changes.

Down-mountain races became popular in Europe and are still the major attraction in any ski meet there. Races with more turns, or slalom races, came along about the same time and since then we've had a battery of new events including giant slalom, super g's, dual slaloms, and so on.

About the 1980s a lot of x-c skiers rediscovered the original Telemark turn and many of them began practicing it using their three-pin cross-country bindings. Some were known as Norpiners because they ventured forth to the Alpine slopes and began practicing their turns there, riding the lift up and doing those graceful turns on their descent. It wasn't too long before many of the Telemarkers discovered that wider touring skis would give more stability. As the Alpine slopes got more firmly packed, it became clear that more control was needed and so the Telemarkers began using those wider touring skis with steel edges on them. Soon, Telemark skis came on the market.

At the same time, it was obvious that more boot control was needed and so stiffer boots were brought into the picture along with cable bindings to replace the three-pin dealies. Some put rigs on their skis to help stabilize the heel when it was needed.

Telemark contests bloomed and these were followed by timed races on courses around poles, using Telemark turns and Telemark equipment throughout. It's probable that more Telemarking events will come onto the scene and it may be that the primary differences between these events and the Alpine events we know today will be that slightly limber boot that allows the heel to lift in the turn . . . and the turns used, of course.

The wheel goes around.

In Sum

If you took a few tries at each of these drills, you would be out there a lot longer than the students at the Putney School. Don't do that much!

You may not have complete choice in the drills you can practice because of snow or track conditions. Or because you have wax or skis that aren't working just right. Or because you just don't want to do some of them. That's fine. Practice what you can, or feel like, and then

TECHNIQUE —
CLASSICAL

go off skiing. If you keep track of your progress, or make notes every once in a while, you may be pleasantly surprised at how far you've come with a bit of practice. I mention making notes because it's often easy to forget where you started in terms of proficiency. If you write it down, there it is and it will give you a good feeling.

For Beginners—Learning Classical

Many beginners have a difficult time learning to ski the classical, or diagonal technique. The timing and coordination between arms and legs does not come naturally. I've found that doing these four drills will teach beginners faster than any other method I know of. I've explained before that one advantage of this learning system is that it concentrates on the arm movements. Many people have better control over their arms than their legs. In addition, these drills help develop the strength and coordination necessary for classical. Here they are, in order.

1. Double-pole in tracks with no strides. This helps to give confidence, build arm strength and coordination, and a feeling for the skis sliding along the snow. Use a slight downhill to begin with, if that makes things easier.

2. Do the one-step double-pole. Slide one ski ahead and double-pole as before. Bring the skis together. Repeat. After several efforts, try getting a little push off the forward ski as you double-pole.

3. Practice the single-pole with no strides, or leg movement. Be sure the poles are slanted backwards so when you push on them, it will propel you in the right direction, down the track. Again, bobbing up and down is OK, especially if it helps propel you and if you can get some good rhythm going. Unless your arms are strong, you will have to do this drill on a slight downhill.

❋ **4.** Finally, slide one ski ahead as in drill number 2, but instead of reaching forward with both poles as in the double-pole, bring only the pole opposite that forward ski ahead. Then pole with that forward arm and try to get a little push off that front ski at the same time. Then use the alternate arm and leg and off you go!

The finished product— diagonal, or classical skiing.

Right arm and left leg begin forward movement.

Full extension as right pole is planted, with weight on the left ski.

TECHNIQUE—
CLASSICAL

Ski Lessons

One of the best ways to learn skiing is to take lessons. There are thousands of good teachers around North America. Almost all ski areas have good staffs ready to help you, no matter what your ability. If you don't like skiing on your own, or have trouble feeling and seeing your own movements, it's just another reason to take lessons.

Relaxed classical skiing in Vermont countryside.

The Professional Ski Instructors Association has a Nordic branch and this group meets regularly to discuss changes in the sport, improved methods for teaching, and any other items that will further the sport. Go with them. They are out to help you and you will be showing support for them if you take some lessons.

You think classical skiing will disappear? No, it looks too good and feels great.

TECHNIQUE —
CLASSICAL

5

Technique — Skating

O NE OF THE puzzles of x-c skiing is why it took so long for racers to catch on to skating. At the 1971 World Junior Championships near Leningrad, the U.S. relay entry of Tim Caldwell, Tom Siebels, and Bill Koch figured out that it was faster to skate the whole stadium area rather than stay in the tracks. They astounded the spectators by this maneuver, but no one picked it up for several more years. In those days we were still using wooden skis and waxing the whole length with x-c wax, so the skis weren't too fast. Snow compaction was not what it is now and often the snow outside the track was very soft and impossible to skate in. But at Leningrad, our team clearly made good time by skating.

The Holmenkollen 50 km race that same season was a waxer's nightmare and found several skiers rewaxing, swapping skis, and dropping out. The East German, Gerhard Grimmer, used a version of the marathon skate instead of stopping to rewax and it must have worked for him because he won the race by seven minutes. This margin is the equivalent of winning a 100 yard dash by 10 yards.

During the winter of 1979, members of the Australian Ski Team came to the states to train and race. It was one of those poor snow years in the east and after we had exhausted our efforts at dryland training in December, we took to ice-skating, with ski poles, no less. The double-poling was fine on the ice, but I remember we felt a bit strange using the diagonal technique. Little did we know how far ahead of the times we were.

Skating eventually came onto the international racing scene around the early '80s. The Finn Paul Siitonen has been given the most

Ice-skating during a snowless December in 1979. Now, when did all this ski-skating begin?

credit for bringing the marathon skate, or half-skate into vogue, and many racers in Europe still refer to this as the Siitonen step. The other skating steps that we know today followed the marathon skate.

No matter. When the countries were beginning to do battle about the marathon skate step during the early '80s, one Norwegian, commenting at a team leaders' meeting before an important competition, said, "Ja, if you want to skate you should go to a skating rink." This neatly summed up the Norwegian attitude toward the marathon skate. It isn't hard to imagine the feelings that the V skate and the other skating steps have generated since.

The FIS battled with the controversy and came in with a compromise solution for the 1984 Games at Sarajevo. The marathon skate—which was the only skate step in use at that time—would be allowed except on certain sections of the course, notably at the very end. In the 15 km, Ove Aunli came breezing into the stadium with a time that was going to land him around fifth place. He began switching tracks for the final downhill, passed the no skating warning

TECHNIQUE—
SKATING

A biathlon racer in the 1984 Sarajevo Olympics. You can see a few marks in the snow left by the marathon skate, but most skiers were using the classical techniques as recently as then.

sign, and promptly skated the rest of the way to the finish. There was a double bit of irony here because Ove was a Norwegian and the Norwegians had taken such a strong stand against skating. To boot, it was left for the Norwegian jury member to notify him of his disqualification. The jury member also happened to be Ove's father-in-law.

Norway was not the only country to stand back from the marathon skate. As the racers came through one section of track in the stadium, about halfway through the race, it was perfectly obvious to the spectators who knew how to skate and who didn't. The Russians and the Finns were particularly awkward and lost time. One couldn't help feeling how much better they would have done had they been skating. But these two countries had also held out very strongly against skating in favor of the classical technique. The controversy has quieted until after the Calgary Olympic Games, but I'm sure it will be picked up again right after that. Meanwhile, feel comfortable in knowing that all the countries are very adept at skating these days.

Skating requires a lot of space, and traffic jams will occur, as evidenced by the pack in a race in Biwabik, Minnesota.

TECHNIQUE —
SKATING

Skating or Classical?

Despite the hard time the skating technique has had gaining acceptance in some countries, there are several advantages to it. In fact, it's difficult to understand all the resistance.

Skating is easier to learn than classical. There is no wax to worry about. How many skiers have been discouraged by the need to wax their skis before going out? And then, on hitting the trails, to find their wax didn't work? This is particularly true in the east where snow conditions vary so much. With skating, you can go on naked, as they say, with bare bottoms. Or, just put some glider wax on the whole length and then go. No matter what anyone tells you, it's a lot easier to wax (or, not wax!) for skating than it is for classical.

Kids especially can pick up skating in no time. It's the best thing that's happened to them since the introduction of x-c equipment. I remember trying to wax our kids' skis when they were two or three years old. (They were a bit slow and couldn't do this themselves!) After a while I found it easier to let them herring-bone, without the benefit of my wax jobs, up the hill in front of the house and schuss back down. They were primarily interested in going fast downhill anyway. They didn't care if they had to climb going back up.

The techniques are easier to learn in skating, given an average amount of strength. In classical skiing you need something to keep your ski from slipping backward. Most people set their kick or purchase wax, or their waxless skis, into the snow and use their arms to stride along. If the skis slip, or your arms aren't strong enough to hold you from slipping, it gets frustrating. In skating, when you edge that ski out to the side, you have good purchase, or as good a platform as you will want to keep you from slipping. That takes away the major problem in learning the classical technique. We take beginning skiers at Putney and they can ski right on to our team the first year—by skating. This never happened with the classical technique.

A trail, or a course prepared for skating, holds up better, or lasts longer than one prepared with tracks for classical skiing. The skaters pack the trail, in a way, every time they go over it. A well-packed skating trail will last indefinitely during a prolonged cold spell. The classical skiers, having to follow tracks, are much more restricted in their use of the snow and the tracks soon wear out, or get glazed or too wobbly, or fill up with leaves, twigs, and dirt. Chalk up another one for skating.

I can tell you my feelings. Right now, skating hurts my joints and I don't enjoy it as much as classical. But I'm trying to improve my strength and endurance, or tolerance for skating, and will just have to see what happens. However, I have defended racers' rights to skate, much to the chagrin of some of my colleagues, who still lean heavily toward traditional skiing.

I always figured that a ski race was a race from one point to another. Racers wore skis and went at it. No one ever dictated when they should double-pole, herring-bone, or whatever. When some hotshots came up with a faster technique, I thought—bully for them. Now, it's clear that races should be separated into the two categories, otherwise everyone would skate since it's faster. So I applaud the efforts to save classical skiing on the racing circuit.

The biggest threat to the elimination of classical skiing comes from the competitors. Racers entering a classical race tend to skate if they think they can get away with it. The best solution to this infringement seems to be stationing a lot of checkers around the course to watch for violations. Do you want to estimate how many checkers you would need on a 15 km course? (On the FIS level, the rules state that in certain checking situations, you need two checkers at each station. One to check, and one to verify the other's work, presumably.) Most clubs don't have the manpower, or the interest, to engage in such demands. It's a sad time when the officials running a race outnumber the competitors. Therefore, clubs tend to take the easy way out and sponsor skating, or freestyle races.

I don't believe that the increased popularity of skating will put a finish to classical skiing on the recreational level. There is no way that will happen. Too many people prefer classical because that's what they learned to do and because it's easier. You can get along at a very low energy level while using some form of the classical technique, but you can't in skating. Skating just requires much more muscle power, even at the slow speeds.

TECHNIQUE—
SKATING

Where does this leave you? I'll tell you. You can do anything you want to. You are really lucky. But there may be some other factors that will sway you in one direction, or another.

Skating is here to stay. If you want to feel in, you better try it. A good procedure is to work it out 50-50 with skating and classical. Some of the racing crowd who prefer skating say that a day of classical is very relaxing and it loosens the muscles. (They don't admit they might have to race in a classical event sometime!)

Some Basic Premises for Skating

Any teacher or coach will tell you that you need to be relaxed in order to skate well. You need good balance and a certain amount of strength.

Many authors of treatises on skating are young and strong, unhindered by gimpy joints, arthritis, middle age, or similar afflictions. So they tell you what to do and how to do it. Unfortunately, they don't consider the possibility that you may not possess enough of something in order to do what they are telling you. This is where I have an advantage. I've been skating for about five years and have learned a lot about personal drawbacks and so I tell you right now, you probably won't be able to do all the drills I offer below for quite a while. But you should merely let them represent a goal, and then go at them.

I'm assuming that you have longer poles—reaching up to your chin, or thereabouts—when you do these drills. You can use your classical skis and boots, but the skis should have only glide wax since any kick wax will slow you too much.

If your poles are too short, you will probably have to lean forward too far. That will put too much weight on the front part of your ski and kill the glide. It will also put an unnecessary strain on your back. You can see that this is an inefficient way to skate.

In most skating techniques, you skate onto a gliding ski and the leg of that gliding ski is bent when you transfer the weight onto it, but then it straightens as you glide. Be sure of this.

Some drills are much more easily done in fast snow conditions. I'll flag them.

It's instructive to go skating in slow snow, especially that cold, crunchy, hard-packed powder. Your skis don't glide very far in these conditions and your weaknesses become quite apparent. For instance, if you lean too far over one ski in the glide, it will come to a screeching halt and you'll nearly go on your nose. Or, if you edge your ski too much when you skate off it, you will slow radically before you can get off that ski. The result will usually be a very weak glide onto the other ski and a loss of momentum. Since the snow is slow, only a correct body position right over the skis will give you decent glide. Otherwise, you'll think you're skiing in sand.

After a few bouts on this cold powder, you may decide to go classical the next time you encounter these conditions.

Except where noted, it's best to begin these drills on flat terrain. If they are too tough here, go to a slight downhill slope. But eventually, you may want to try them on uphill sections. This will take patience, training, and strength.

In order to skate, you will need a well-packed, firm surface.

Drills for Skating

If you have done a lot of ice-skating, these drills may be a piece of cake. If you have strong legs for whatever reason, that will help too. If you are a weakling, like me, take on these drills slowly and deliberately.

❄️ 1. Begin with the marathon skate. You need flat tracks for this one. Keep one ski in the track, splay the other ski to the side, and push off it as you double-pole. Continue. It's a bit similar to the scooter drill for classical. Learn to skate from both sides. In general, it's easier to vee the ski on the lower side of the track.

TECHNIQUE —
SKATING

❄ **2.** Practice skating with no poles. A smooth, slight downhill section is a good place to start. Fast snow also helps here. Work on your balance first by making short movements, then begin to push off or skate harder so that you glide longer on each ski. When you get this down, skate back up the hill, trying for a bit of glide with each skating step. Begin trying to narrow the V, or the angle between the two skis. The wider the angle, the more distance you travel to the side; the narrower the angle, the more distance you travel in the direction of the track, or the course. It's worthwhile experimenting or persisting at this early stage because as you get more proficient, you will be happy with a narrower V.

This may be the most important drill you can do. Too many coaches have been putting emphasis on the upper body movements and have neglected the strongest limbs we have. If you develop the balance and strength to skate without poles, your technique while using poles will be better.

Now practice skating with just one pole. Be sure you can do this drill with either pole. If you get on a slight sidehill slope, you will begin to get a feel for which side you prefer using the stronger skating stroke on.

❄ **3.** Do the diagonal skate, or the diagonal V as it's sometimes called. In this one you use your poles one at a time and in the same way you use them doing the classical, or diagonal technique.

Once again, we reach a crucial point in the development of your technique. If you are not careful here and pole too vigorously too soon, your body will tend to stiffen up and the power from the skating leg will be cut off. Don't buy this talk that skating is 60% upper body strength. Instead, be sure you are getting a good, firm push off that power leg and that it continues as you pole with one arm.

At this point it would be a good idea to check your leg power by going back to skating without poles. Are you getting just as much leg power with the diagonal as you do without poles? If so, proceed.

The diagonal skate on a slight uphill. This technique requires a fair amount of stretching and some good timing with the leg and arm thrusts.

The push off the right ski onto the left . . .

TECHNIQUE—
SKATING

. . . as the left pole is positioned for the next push. Notice forward recovery of right ski.

Right pole recovery as push on left pole and left ski continues.

THE NEW
CROSS-COUNTRY
SKI BOOK

Power on right pole and push off right ski puts Zack's weight onto his left ski, which becomes the gliding ski.

Cycle is complete.

TECHNIQUE —
SKATING

Ace Photographer

I thought a long time about taking pictures of skating and how to best present them. Shooting a sequence of diagonal or classical pictures from the side shows the viewer quite a bit. All the movements are in one plane, or direction. At least, they are supposed to be. With skating we bring in another dimension since the skis, poles, and even the body are splayed out to the side. With pictures taken from the side, it is easy to lose the true directions the skis and poles and body take because of the foreshortening. I figured that taking some shots from above would help this problem a great deal.

Hiring a helicopter was out of the question. I considered leaning over one of the long bridges on Interstate 91 and zooming in on a skier below skating along on top of the ice on a river. But given my record with the state police, I quickly gave up on that idea. Then I realized the answer was at home, so I packed the snow next to our ski jump trestle and climbed up—see photo—and took the pictures of Zachary from there.

It wasn't as easy as that. The first shots were taken on a sunny day and the shadows were monstrous and too distracting. I waited for a week for an overcast day and shot again. A bigger disaster yet. I had an inferior camera and used the wrong exposure. Unbelievable as it may seem, I had to wait for 10 days to get another cloudy day to shoot. In Vermont, mind you! By that time I had in my grip a better camera and you now have the results.

The overhead sequences were taken from the top of the ski jump, and the sideviews were taken from a field a few hundred meters away. I wanted the pictures to be in synch, as if I had taken them simultaneously at the same location with two different cameras. The best I could do was to ask Zach to ski at the same speed (so the motordrive camera would record the specific movements at the same time) and skate off the same side to begin with, for all the sequences.

Author in top of Putney ski jump getting overhead skating shots.

Then I hoped I could match them up. The secret's out. That's how we did it. I owe most of the credit to the skier, who happens to be quite good technically. And patient as well.

❄ 4.   Practice the V-1 skate, which is double-poling as you skate off one ski—say the left—gliding on the right while you recover the poles and skate off the right ski, then double-poling again while you skate off the left ski. If the track is tipped slightly to one side, you will find it easier and more efficient to pole onto the ski going with the downhill slope—which is why you need to be able to do the V-1 to both sides. Practice.

As usual, this is most easily done on a slight downhill slope, but eventually, as you gain strength and balance, you should move to the flats and then the uphills.

I'll say it once more. Don't concentrate so much on the double-poling motion that you forget to use your legs properly; that is, with good power. It's easy to fall into the bad habit of leaning onto the poles, tightening up throughout the length of your body, and losing the push from that skating leg.

TECHNIQUE—
SKATING

The V-1 from the side and as seen from overhead. Note the fairly upright position throughout. Beginning of poling motion with the weight on the right ski.

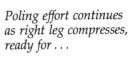

*Poling effort continues
as right leg compresses,
ready for . . .*

TECHNIQUE—
SKATING

. . . its thrust, which sends Zack gliding over and onto his left ski.

The follow-through while gliding on the left ski.

Midpoint of recovery. Arms and right ski swing forward as glide continues.

Weight shifts to right ski as cycle is completed. See first photo.

TECHNIQUE—
SKATING

❅ **5.** Practice the V-2 skate. In this one you double-pole as you skate off each ski. You'll need to move quickly and keep your body weight slightly more forward than in the V-1 skate. The poling motion is not as long. The V-2 is very fast and quite tiring as well.

So you should start slowly at it and here's a good drill. Set up some sticks, or poles at regular intervals—maybe 12–15 feet apart at the beginning—and do the V-2 around them. The only rule is this: you get one double-pole motion and one skate for each stick you pass. See how slowly you can do it, then move the sticks farther apart, or stagger them as you improve.

The V-2 may come on as a premier technique for the supermen in x-c. Right now, most skiers lack the balance and strength to do the V-2 for protracted lengths. But that will change.

Two racers in different stages of the skating technique.

The V-2 from the side and from overhead. The movements and body positions here are very similar to those of the V-1 technique but are shortened and speeded up a bit. The increased speed does not show in these shots but a careful study will reveal shorter poling motions, for instance.

TECHNIQUE —
SKATING

Poling while weight transfers from left to right ski.

Follow-through and glide onto the right ski.

TECHNIQUE — SKATING

Left ski and arms begin recovery with weight still on right side.

Left ski is still recovering as poling and push off the right ski begins.

TECHNIQUE—
SKATING

Now the weight and glide is shifted to the left ski, which is Veed out.

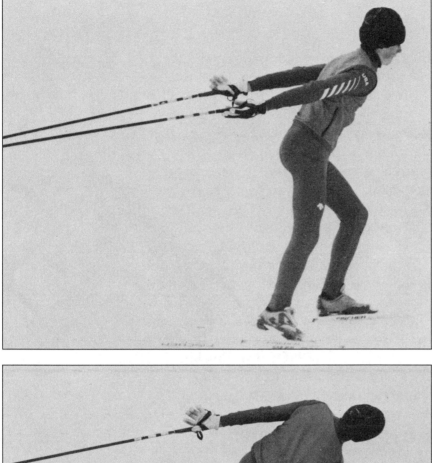

Follow-through onto the left gliding ski.

TECHNIQUE –
SKATING

Uphill Skating

✻ **6.** Later on, as you gain proficiency with the diagonal skate, you will find it very useful for skating uphills. The reason it works so well is that your speed does not vary much from ski to ski and therefore you don't lose your momentum. By comparison, when using the V-1 on the uphills, you get a good initial burst of speed as you double-pole and skate off one ski, but by the time you are ready to pole and skate off that same ski again, you have slowed markedly and have to get all hitched up again for another power stroke.

It's on the uphills that you have to do something different or else you'll stall out, like I do. If you don't bring your foot forward and underneath you quickly, you won't get very much glide. So make a conscious effort to pick up that foot more than usual and bring it up. You can think of lifting your knee, or upper leg more. Fast snow helps too.

Another trick to try is this: drop your butt a bit, or sit back more than you normally do on the flat. You may not be able to straighten your legs as you skate onto each ski, but if you maintain some momentum, you are doing it right. Don't be surprised if your muscles burn a little bit when you do this one.

In terms of pure speed, the best way to skate up a hill may be by using the V-2, but there are not a lot of skiers in the world who are strong enough to do this just now, so I'd advise the diagonal skate for you. And if you don't get any glide from this step, just tell the folks watching that you are doing the herring-bone.

✻ **7.** Try the passgang V. It may be a new one. It's fun. In this one you reach forward with the arm and ski on the same side, instead of alternating as in the diagonal V. Some skiers use this technique on uphills and prefer it to the diagonal.

Beginning skiers learning the classical sometimes use the passgang instead of the so-called diagonal. A practiced eye can pick up this fault of moving the arm and leg on the same side of the body forward instead of moving one arm and the leg opposite it forward. The passgang itself is OK as a classical technique until you get to a hill. Then when you reach forward with the same arm and leg, you will slip. In fact, the best way to break skiers of the passgang habit is to get them to try and ski up a hill using it. The only way they can really manage will be to revert to diagonal, or using alternate limbs.

The reason the passgang V works on uphills is that your ski is edged and that keeps you from slipping back.

❄ **8.** Practice what I will call the V-1½ skate. That would be double-poling off every third step. Double-pole and skate off the left ski, glide onto the right, skate off the right and glide onto the left, skate off the left and glide onto the right, then skate and pole off the right ski. Repeat the sequence and eventually skate and double-pole off the left ski. You'll shake your head a few times before you get this one down, but it's marvelous for the coordination, timing, and balance. Fast snow is best here.

❄ **9.** You can make up some of your own rhythms for this one. Try three V-2s, three V-1s, throw in a few diagonal skates, some passgang, and start all over again. By doing these different techniques sequentially, you will begin to get a good feel for shifting your body position and at the same time will learn a lot about the best technique for a given section of track, or for given snow conditions.

It's always good to try and analyze these things on your own. What you learn will stay with you longer than information someone might pass on to you, information that might be wrong, by the way.

TECHNIQUE—
SKATING

❄ **10.** If you have a friend who is near in ability to you, it's good practice to take turns following each other closely. Compare skates or kicks, distances you glide on each ski, the angles your skis make with the straight-ahead direction, the ease with which you go up hills, and so on. Shift leads. Talk about it. Figure out the reasons for the differences. Swap skis, if that's possible. Have a clinic. Help each other. You'll learn a lot.

Summary of Similarities and Differences between Classical and Skating

To be sure, both techniques, classical and skating, require skis, boots, bindings, poles, and decent snow surfaces and tracks. Let's agree that both techniques are skiing. But the connoisseurs of the sport have different sets of equipment for each technique. I have already pointed out that changing the poles is really the only thing you need to do when first changing from one technique to the other. When you get more proficient, you may want a separate set of equipment for each technique.

Since skating poles are longer, the poling motion is different. The arms go through a longer range of motion, beginning with the hands and elbows much higher than in classical skiing. The hands start above the head and the elbows are sometimes raised higher than the shoulders at the beginning of the stroke. (This depends largely on the length of your poles.) This forces more of a pulling motion, similar to when doing a chin-up, to initiate the poling stroke in skating. However, the arm poling motion to the rear is not as complete as in the classical. Despite this shortening, the tempos for skating are generally slower since the arm movements take longer. And arm movements determine tempo.

In classical the hands usually start above the shoulders but I prefer a technique where no real poling pressure is put on the forearms until the hands are slightly below the shoulders.

The weight shift over the gliding ski is clear when seen from behind. In the lower two photos, the push off the right ski is completed. In the top photo, the right ski tail crosses the left ski in the recovery phase. Excellent technique.

TECHNIQUE—
SKATING

Ice-Skating

Skating began for good around 1980 when Paul Siitonen figured out that the marathon skate, or half-skate, was a lot faster than plain diagonal (or, now known as classical) skiing. From there it was just a matter of time before the V step, using both skis instead of one to skate, came along.

At the beginning there was a fair amount of controversy about the equipment best suited for skating and some skiers even tried using one long pole, much like a Venetian boatman pushing along the canals. Soon it became apparent that shorter skis were easier to handle and as snow compaction improved, stiffer skis proved to be an advantage.

The International Ski Federation stepped in quickly and dictated that poles could be no longer than the racer's height, or shorter than the hip. Skis had to be at least equal to the racer's height but could be no longer than 230 cm.

One can understand why the federation mandated rules for the equipment because the story might have continued like this: soon the crowds and organizers were clamoring for faster times on the courses, more excitement and all that. So the course preparation crews began to ice the snow after it had been packed. This led the skiers to use shorter skis with sharper edges in order to maintain decent control. Course preparation continued to improve and soon the courses looked as smooth as a skating rink after a Zamboni has made its passes. New equipment kept pace, and it wasn't long before skiers were using shoes, or boots, with nothing more than blades attached, much like speed skates. Thus, cross-country speed skating was invented.

Riding a flat ski in both techniques is so important that skiers who are able to do this in one technique usually can do it in the other technique and always seem to be just a bit more efficient than those who flop from edge to edge while gliding.

In both techniques, the skiers who can transpose the most energy in the direction of the tracks are going to be more efficient. Imagine doing a wide V as you skate, or bobbing from side to side as you do the classical technique—you won't be as efficient as the skier who directs more effort down the track.

6

Waxing

*T*HERE IS little doubt that the waxing of x-c skis is a subject that contains more stories, more hocus-pocus, more pseudo-scientific approaches, more information, and more controversy than any other phase of this sport.

When I started skiing in the '30s and early '40s the only wax available to me was from candles. Some of us began to try and analyze the different colors of candles and I'm sure it did not amount to much. Was the blue candle really faster in powder than the red one? We took a giant step forward with the introduction of the Sohm's Orange that I have already referred to. That stuff really helped one from slipping back and we used it on downhill skis when we took long tours. There was also Sohm's Red and Sohm's Blue, but we used them primarily for speed waxes in slalom and downhill races. Rub it on and smooth it out—that was the method.

World War II was in progress during my early years of skiing and one result was that wax from Europe was virtually unavailable. However, soon after the war, Bob Smith-Johanssen, the son of the famed Jack Rabbitt Johanssen, came out with the first two-wax system I know of. He produced a wet snow wax and a dry snow wax and during the late '40s and early '50s we used these with quite good success on our x-c skis.

In 1948, after my college coach, Walter Prager, came back from coaching the U.S. Olympic Alpine Team, we took another step forward and started ironing wax onto the skis. Heretofore we had always rubbed it on and then corked it in. One of the first Alpine races I was in that year found us using good old Sohm's Red, ironed in from tip to tail. This was revolutionary and we thought our skis fairly flew over the snow. The next refinement was melting all the Alpine waxes together in a pot and painting them on in steps, beginning at the back of the ski. We used long, thin steps for powder snow and colder conditions, and shorter, thicker steps for wetter, warmer snow. We needed the thicker steps to break up the suction between wet snow and the skis.

At about the same time, we got hold of some Swix x-c waxes from Sweden and some Ostbye waxes from Norway and these were the first waxes I ever used that were specifically designed for cross-country. At one college carnival, Walter, who was an outstanding waxer, layered on coats of Blue Swix and Ostbye Mix for the x-c race. When we asked him what he used, he grinned and said, "Ja, Svix, Mix, Svix." The idea was that the Swix would wear off exposing the Mix when we needed it, and the Mix would wear off and expose the bottom layer of Swix when we needed that. By gosh, it worked too!

Specialized Alpine waxes (we didn't call them glider waxes then) were not available during the war either. But when I got to college, I found that no one was using candles, so I shipped mine back to my brother Pete, who was at school in Putney. Instead, everyone used Lebanon White, named after a nearby town. Lebanon White came in several different brands, as I recall. There was Esso, and Gulf, and maybe Kitchen Pride, or something like that, and it was used mostly in making jams. Yeah, it was canning paraffin.

We used Lebanon White a lot for ski-jumping too and it was then that we developed the business of rubbing it on rough for wet snow—again, to help break the suction between the snow and the ski bottoms—and putting it on very thin for cold, powder snow. That approach is as good today as it was then.

One thing we spent a lot of time at in those days was burning in pine tar on those wood-bottomed x-c skis. Whenever one of our coaches wanted to get us out of his hair, he would send us packing to pine-tar our skis, especially the night before a competition. When we were on the road, staying in some of the older New England milltown hotels, we were usually given the boiler room to complete our assigned task. Now, I marvel at the faith the management had in

WAXING

us, working in the bottom of a big, old wooden structure with gasoline blowtorches. We loved the smell and often spent hours at a time just waving the flame back and forth across the ski bottom, watching the tar bubble while taking in those lousy fumes. I've thought that if tarring skis had been good training, I probably would have been an Olympic medalist. But it probably had an adverse effect of clogging my lungs. I could smell the stuff lots of times out there on the course during a race when I got breathing hard.

Our first try at getting more speed for our x-c skis was by using a faster x-c wax on the tips and tails and a different one, which would climb better, under the foot. This method of waxing—using x-c climbing wax on the whole ski and not any glider wax—lasted well into the '70s. For instance, in 1968 at the Grenoble Olympics, we waxed two different kinds of blue klister for the 50 km event—Swix under the foot, since it had better climb, and Rode on the tips and tails since it was faster. By using so much klister, we kept the wax companies in business.

The amazing thing is that we rarely used paraffin on the tips and tails of our cross-country skis. The first time I used it was at a prep school championship in the mid-fifties at the Breadloaf Campus of Middlebury College. We had a big storm brewing during the race and the precipitation was coming down in all forms—plain snow, cornmeal-like snow, sleet, rain, you name it. I mixed up a can of silver Alpine wax with some Lebanon White and painted it on the tips and tails of the x-c skis—right there in what used to be the little timing shack. I'll never forget the look on the faces of the officials when they saw what I was doing. I know they had never seen that before. Nor had I! Our racers still iced up a bit, but not as much as their competitors who had x-c wax from tip to tail. On the downhill sections, our skis were so fast that some of the guys went into the woods, thus negating any wax advantage we might have had.

I knew that method had possibilities. Hindsight is always 20-20, as they say, and I feel like something of a dummy for not having used paraffin on the tips and tails of x-c skis for a long time after that race at Middlebury. I guess I figured it was worthwhile only in extreme situations when almost anything else one used would ice up. But we waxers never liked to admit that we couldn't find a wax that would not ice. We had a lot of pride. So I suppose that was another reason we were reluctant to use paraffin on the tips and tails. We just didn't think we needed it.

Waxing moved ahead during the late '50s and early '60s, mainly by virtue of having many more brands of Alpine and x-c wax on the market. It began to get confusing and everyone was looking for something better than the next fellow.

Waxless Skis

The first attempt I know of at producing waxless skis in this country was made by two brothers, Bob and Bill Bennett. They bought those fishscale strips from the Attenhofer Ski Company hoping to make Alpine skis steadier on downhill runs and to eliminate the need for waxing x-c's. In the summer of 1967, they hired Mike Gallagher to fly to South America to test all sorts of skis with the fishscale strips on. Mike noticed that the skis seemed to climb well, but that they didn't really help the Alpine skis going downhill. Eventually, the design was bought by another company and used exclusively for cross-country skis.

After the fishscale design, there was a proliferation of other designs, many of which have been modified or discarded. There have been other "plain" bottoms developed with special features that aid in purchase, or climb, along the way and at one time, half or more of the x-c market has been in so-called waxless skis.

Fiberglass

In 1974 when the top racers began using fiberglass skis in the major competitions, we reached another milestone. The correct waxing of fiberglass skis was slightly difficult at first because most skiers used the same methods they had been using on wood skis. Quite often the wax slipped, or wore off easily. As the racers solved these difficulties by using softer waxes than they normally would for wood skis, or by using binders to help hold the wax, the manufacturers changed the bottoms so they were faster and held the wax better.

It wasn't long before racers began using glide wax on the tips and tails instead of the traditional x-c grip wax. During the late '70s, there were several clinics given in the U.S. on the art of glide waxing. Some of the coaches from Scandinavia, feeling they were behind in this aspect, came to clinics in this country. I vividly recall one approach taken by the waxmasters of the day, just to show you one of the myths.

The ski bottoms were likened to the pores of one's skin and when heated with hotwax ironed in, would open up and "accept" the wax. Clinic-goers were told to hotwax tips and tails in a warm room, bottoms up, naturally, so the wax could fill in those pores, and to leave the skis in that position overnight. (Remember, this was the '70s.) Then the skis were to be scraped practically clean, cooled, and used. When those pores in the ski bottoms were exposed to the cold snow, you can guess what happened next. The pores contracted and squeezed a thin film of wax out and that's what made the skis glide so well. No one thought to ask why those pores would not "accept" or soak up water in the track on warm days and thus make the skis quite slow.

Since then, the more accepted theory is that the ski bottoms, when hotwaxed, combine chemically with the wax and form a fast surface after most of the wax has been scraped off.

Sintered Bases

Now, the skis with the new, sintered bases really do soak up the wax as described above, according to the latest theory. I'm told that a new sintered base will "accept" up to 15–20 grams of wax when it's melted, or ironed in. The wax experts will admit that those older, "extruded" bases do not soak up wax. Since bases are either extruded or sintered, it's worth your while to find out which you are getting.

Even without any of these theories, anyone who made the transition from wood skis to fiberglass knows that the fiberglass skis are much faster, even when left unwaxed.

Some New Methods

In the early '80s, members of the U.S. Team brought back a do-it-yourself method for making waxless skis out of regular plain-bottomed fiberglass skis. That was done by roughing up (or abrading) the kicker zone under the foot by using some rough sandpaper or a special tool, and then applying silicon spray. These skis were (and still are) especially effective for those marginal conditions around freezing when almost any wax is apt to ice up. That's what I should have used at Middlebury in 1955!

I'm not clear when rilling, or structuring, ski bottoms . . . putting longitudinal grooves in them . . . came in. One theory for this rilling is that when skis slide over snow, a very thin film of water is created and if there are grooves in your ski base, the water will follow these grooves and create less friction between the snow and the ski. Like the ads you see for tires on TV. The warmer and wetter the snow, the more you need to rill them if you want fast skis. I'm not especially fond of the theory but the system works. More about the method later.

Ski-skating came along during the early eighties and it has had a profound effect on waxing. Now, when we skate we're right back to where I was during the '30s when all I used was paraffin the whole length. No more kick wax! Well, I should have been able to predict that one.

At this writing there is a big move to preserve classical (or diagonal) skiing on the international level and that will undoubtedly sift down to the recreation level . . . if there is a need to preserve classical! Kick wax, or climbing wax, will again be popular. But meanwhile the wax companies are busily preparing new kinds of glider wax to be used for skating. Their main features are durability and speed, of course.

Every time there is a major change in x-c, it means something more is going to be done about waxing. Many x-c'ers already feel beleaguered with waxing and can only groan with each new development. I gave up on wax charts a few editions ago because they were outdated before we could get them into print in book form. So I sympathize with you and this time have broken waxing up for four groups, or classes of skiers. The first group is one that practices a bit less than the basics, and the groups go on from there. Plug yourself in to one group and ignore the higher classifications, if you want to.

Group 1. This is the group that never, I mean never, waxes. They use waxless skis and do classical skiing, or they may use waxable skis but go skating every time out.

There are no hints I can give this group about waxing, but I will tell you that your ski bottoms may get clogged, or dirty and greasy after a while and will not function as well as when they were new. They may turn a bit white and while a lot of purists claim this is very bad, I have never noticed severe effects from this condition.

Sub-group 1A. This group of skiers uses mainly waxless skis but tries to keep them operating well by cleaning the ski bottoms when they get dirty, or clogged. They also use hotwax.

Get hold of some wax remover and wipe the skis clean when they get dirty. On most waxless skis, the section that provides the grip should be left unwaxed, so you don't do anything but clean this when it gets dirty. However, the plain part of the ski bottom—usually the tips and tails—should be hotwaxed occasionally. If it gets that white look, it's a good time to hotwax. You can hold the bottom to the light and sometimes see if it needs wax.

There are a lot of glider waxes you can use for this purpose. To keep it simple, get hold of two—one for cold snow and one for warmer snow around freezing, or above. Making sure the skis are clean and dry, and that you're inside, hold the wax against an iron set for wool, or at about 140°F, and melt a strip onto each side of the goove. Then iron it in just as you might iron handkerchiefs. After the wax cools, scrape it with a plastic scraper—it's OK to move outside now—being sure to clean out the groove and the edges as well. (The grooves are there to improve tracking, or going in a straight line. If they are plugged, the ski will slide too easily from side to side. And if you leave wax on the edges, it will grab every time you edge your ski.)

You melt the wax on and then scrape it off? When I first heard this several years ago, my reaction was incredulous. I paid good money for that wax and we've always skied on a good coat of wax. Now, you scrape it off! I'm sorry. It just works much better as a very, very thin coat. The main advantage of melting the wax may be that chemical reaction that takes place between the wax and the base of the ski.

You can always save the shavings and use them again if you're on a tight budget.

Group 2. This is the group that uses waxable skis and has settled for a two-wax system for kick, or purchase. It also uses glider wax on tips and tails and applies it as described above.

There are quite a few two-wax systems, one invariably for colder, powder snow and the other for snow in warmer temperatures. As usual, it's easiest when you wax inside with clean and dry skis. Rub the wax on under the midsection for a length of about two feet. Then smooth it by corking.

In general, a thicker coat of wax will provide more kick than a thinner coat. Also, thinner coats work best on cold snow and slightly thicker coats on warmer snow. But none of the coats will work optimally unless you put a lot of energy into really smoothing them out with the cork. There should be a shine to the finished job.

You will have to experiment with the length of your kick wax strip to see how long it should be. If your skis slip, try added thickness. If they still slip, lengthen the kicker strip. If they still slip, you probably need a softer wax.

On the other hand, if your skis feel slow and draggy, you may have a kicker strip that is too long. Or, you may have a wax that is too soft. If the kicker strip wears off at the front or back of the section, yet continues to give you pretty good purchase, use this as an indicator for the positioning of your next wax job.

Group 3. This is the group that has begun a study of waxing and usually has the skis ready with the appropriate waxes—one glider and one kick wax for classical skiing, or just glide wax for skating— chosen from one brand's line.

You will probably have the optimum results for the amount of effort you put into waxing. Get hold of the complete line of wax put out by one company and read the directions they provide for the application and use of their products. Then, using the information above and the hints on kick waxes below, go to it. The Swix company probably has the most complete line.

Group 4. This is the eager group that owns two, three, or four complete lines of wax and has about every device known to very serious waxers, including rilling tools, various metal and plastic scrapers, brushes, several different grits and varieties of sandpaper, books, notes, journals, wax charts, thermometers, snow-testing devices, radios to call to higher or lower elevations to get a check on conditions, and so on. If you are in this group, you may be headed for one of the national teams as waxing adviser and certainly don't need advice here.

I hope the waxes you have don't go out of style too fast. I used to belong to Group 4 and one day when I was waxing for the U.S. Team, I found something that worked well, but the problem was there wasn't another tube of that stuff in the whole country. So, what good was it? I had just built up some false hopes on the part of the racers I was trying to help.

Well, what did your team wax?

THE NEW
CROSS-COUNTRY
SKI BOOK

Now, when someone asks me for waxing advice, I begin by asking them what waxes do they have at their disposal. Then we go on from there.

Kick Waxes — Hard

As before, you should determine the length of your kicker wax strip, but now you may have as many as 10 different kick waxes to choose from. Here follows a whole lot of good advice to observe when you are in this group.

1. Be sure your skis are well-cleaned and dry before you apply the wax. Don't put glider wax on the kicker section of your ski. Kick wax will not adhere well over glider wax. Simply rub the wax on and cork it in.

An alternative method for applying hardwax is to melt it on by holding it against an iron, and then using the iron to smooth it. It's faster than applying it by hand and corking it in, but you are apt to do a messier job because the wax will spill over onto the sidewalls of the skis and into the groove. If it is not cleaned off, it will hold you up, especially if you try to skate a few steps, or do some step turns.

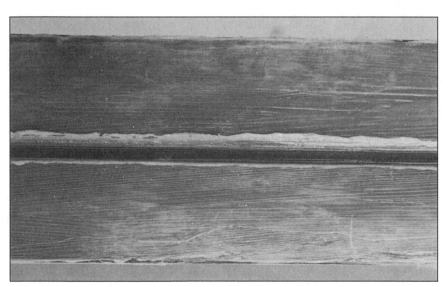

A finished job of ironed-in hardwax.

WAXING

2. K.I.S.S., which stands for "Keep it simple, stupid." I wish I had followed this advice lots of times. Try one wax rather than two or three. If some mysterious combination works by chance, you will probably never be able to duplicate it. If you have a choice of 8–10 kicker waxes, you ought to be able to find one wax that works, especially by varying the length of your kicker and the thickness of the wax.

3. Use hardwaxes for new snow and different forms of powder snow, and klisters for snow that has melted and frozen again.

4. Despite having as many as 10 waxes to choose from, beware. It's not all peaches and cream. One of the problems that comes up follows: some wax companies specify the temperature ranges for their waxes and some overlap, some have very small ranges, and you think, good—that makes it simple. However, a lot of thermometers are off by a couple of degrees and if you happen on to one of these and use it to help make your wax selection, you may be disappointed. It's better to build a feel for the snow, the temperature, and the wax that works. This takes practice, and a bit of time.

5. More problems can crop up. Most ski waxes recommend air temperature ranges and while it's true that snow is usually colder than the air, and there may be a consistent difference between the snow and air temperatures, there are some days when this just ain't so. Imagine a few very cold days that send snow temperatures plummeting, followed by a nice, warm morning, with the temperature going right up toward the freezing mark. The snow will be very cold for quite a while, especially in shady sections, even though the air temperature may be approaching 30°F. So if you used a soft blue wax in these conditions, it would probably drag a lot, and wear quite quickly.

I always like to compare the snow temperature with the air temperature and go on from there. That's not all, while I'm at it. The amount of moisture in the snow is very important too. The more moisture, the softer the wax you will need. You can have very cold snow that requires a blue wax because of its moisture content, or may require a cold green wax because it is so dry.

I'm not trying to make this complicated. But it will help if you think about these factors.

6. If in doubt between two waxes, use the harder wax first, then cover it with the softer wax, if necessary. However, don't think that using a harder wax in moist snow will make you faster. For instructional purposes you might try a cold green wax, polished so it shines, on some wet snow some day. You'll find the suction between your skis' wax job and the snow is remarkable. As we say, your kick wax may be slow, but at least it will slip.

One way to add a little kick out on the trail.

WAXING

7. When the snow is older, or has been groomed quite a bit, use a wax that is slightly softer than the temperature calls for. Snow crystals in this condition are not as sharp and therefore a slightly softer or warmer wax will work better.

8. You're all waxed and out on the trail and the skis begin to slip, or ice up. What then?

Let's hope you have looked ahead and have researched the weather enough to know it's going to warm up, or get colder, and that you have the next softer or harder kick wax you will need. If that's too risky for you, take along one softer wax and one harder. In addition, you should have a scraper, a cork, a small piece of paraffin (Lebanon White does nicely), and a piece of terrycloth, or something absorbent to dry the ski before you add wax.

For icing, it's usually best to scrape the ski, dry it with the cloth, and rub on some paraffin. Go! If you slip too much after this, dry the ski again and use your harder kick wax.

For slipping, dry the ski and apply the next softer kick wax. Cork it, of course.

Kick Waxes—Klister

I've helped to wax a lot of skis and toward the end of a season here at Putney, I usually have a fair idea of each skier's requirements. But it takes a couple of months for me to figure them out. We have a fun relay race at Mount Hermon School each spring where everyone races and it's always klister skiing. When there are 20–30 skiers to wax, you just don't hand out 10–15 tubes of klister and stand back. Because chaos would ensue. Instead, I often apply the klister to each pair of skis and vary the length and thickness according to the skiers' needs. I let the skiers rub it out. It's not that I don't like rubbing in klister, but I'm in education, you know.

The best way to rub it out is by using the heel of your palm. The klister is spread easier if it's warm.

Some finicky people use corks to smooth the klister but they usually pay the consequences when the cork comes in contact with everything imaginable afterwards.

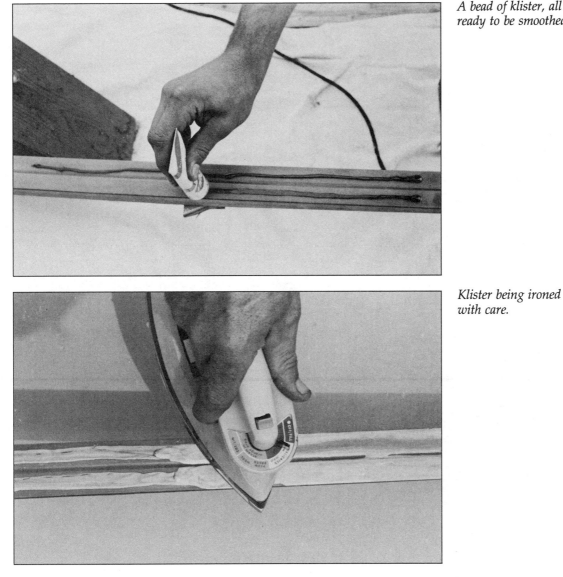

A bead of klister, all ready to be smoothed!

Klister being ironed with care.

You can squeeze klister onto the skis and iron it in too, if you have a very good, light touch. Otherwise, most of the klister will end up in the groove and on the sidewalls.

A finished klister job will be about as thick as a good coat of paint on the clapboards of a house.

WAXING

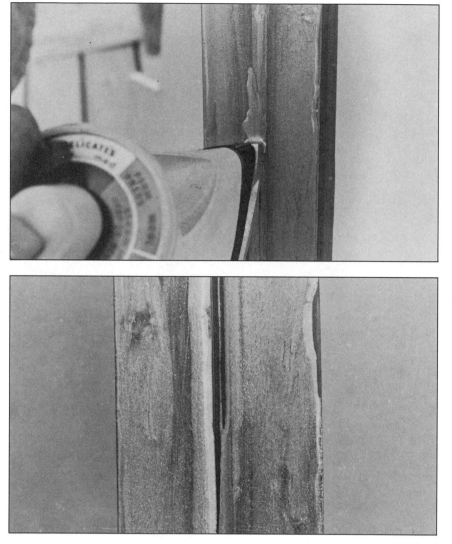

Scooping the klister out of the groove.

The finished klister job, all ironed in.

Binder Wax

Binder wax used to be more necessary than it is now. It is a special wax with extreme wearing qualities used to help hold on kicker waxes in abrasive conditions. Used alone, it's slow as death.

With so much snow grooming now, there is not so much need for binders because the snow crystals are softer, more rounded, and less abrasive. (You'd be less abrasive too, if you went through those snow tillers a couple of times.)

But if you need a binder because of harsh snow conditions, heat the tube by holding it against a warm iron and daub the stuff on the kicker zone of the skis. Iron it in, cool it, and wax as usual over the top of the binder.

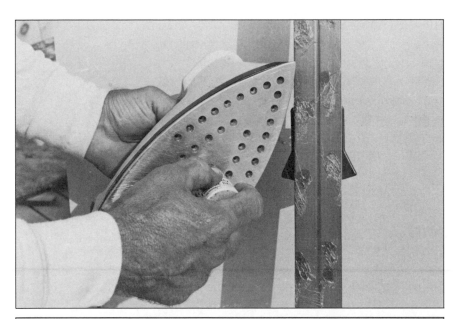

Binder wax being warmed on the iron and dabbed onto the ski.

Binder being ironed in.

WAXING

How to Clean the Skis

Hardwaxes for cold snow are most easily scraped off when the wax is cold. Do it outside. Those softer hardwaxes may come off easier outside too. It's a toss-up between outside and inside. After you get as much scraped off as you can, it's time to bring them in and use a wax solvent to get the remains.

Klisters are a bit messier and need replacing more often than hardwaxes. To clean, I usually start with a scraper and work until the stuff rolls over and over and eventually under the scraper itself. Then I reach for the nearest can of gas, soak a rag with it, and wipe the ski as clean as I can. Most people will recommend you use a wax solvent for this job. I've heard lectures on the dangers of gasoline. There are traces of oil in there that can slow the base. And those chemicals in gas just don't react well with the ski bottoms. All that stuff. I still use gas because it's a lot less expensive, but I do follow it with a wax solvent to clean up the remains of the klister and any impurities there might be in the gas.

All solvents I know of are highly flammable. Use them with care in places where there is plenty of air and dispose of the rags properly.

A few years back, the U.S. Team coaches hit on a marvelous solvent for waxes of all kinds. It was something used quite a bit in photography and I forget the name of it. It worked very well. Two years later I read an article about the cancer-causing properties of this particular chemical. So much for that. I wasn't worried too much because I had stuck with my gasoline. Unleaded, of course.

Preparing New Skis

To get the best performance from your new skis, you should prepare the bottoms. If they don't come already rilled (see below) and ready for whatever waxes you may want to use, you should work them over yourself.

The first thing to do is check them for flatness by seeing if there is any light between a square metal scraper and the ski bottom as you drag it along. Some skis come with a slightly convex or concave bottom, which should be flattened. If they need work, secure them well in a vise and scrape the spots that are out of square. Naturally, be sure your scraper is straight. You can check it by lining it up along something like a T-square. If the scraper is not straight, file it and check it again.

After scraping, the bottoms should be sanded smooth with silicon carbide sandpaper, using different grits, beginning with the rougher, maybe around #100, and progressing to #160 or #180. Or, use #100 and finish up with something like a Scotch-Brite pad. The serious racers have every grit from around #80 to #300 and use a lot of them, according to the snow conditions. The rougher stuff is used for wet, warm snow and the finer grits are used for cold, powdery snow.

After sanding, wipe them clean with a rag or some special wax company paper and then brush them with one of those brushes especially designed for this purpose. Melt in some glider wax on the tips and tails if you plan to use kick wax, or on the whole ski if you plan on skating. Then, scrape most of it off with a plastic scraper, leaving just a very thin film. At this point, most hotshots brush the glide wax and go skiing.

Rilling

Rilling the base is most often recommended for skating skis and when the snow is wet. In wet snow, according to the prevailing theory, there is more water build-up between the ski and the snow, and the water causes a lot of suction, or slow skis. The rilling will create those longitudinal grooves for the water to follow, or escape through. We used to rill the wax on our downhill skis to create this good effect, but that was when we skied on much thicker coats of wax. Now the glide wax on x-c skis is so thin that it's necessary to rill the base instead. And before you rill the base, it must be absolutely clean and free of wax.

The eager skiers rill their bases using special rilling tools available from some companies. The tools come with different sized rillers and by now you should be able to guess what is wanted—deeper grooves for wet snow and finer, shallower grooves for cold, powder snow. If

WAXING

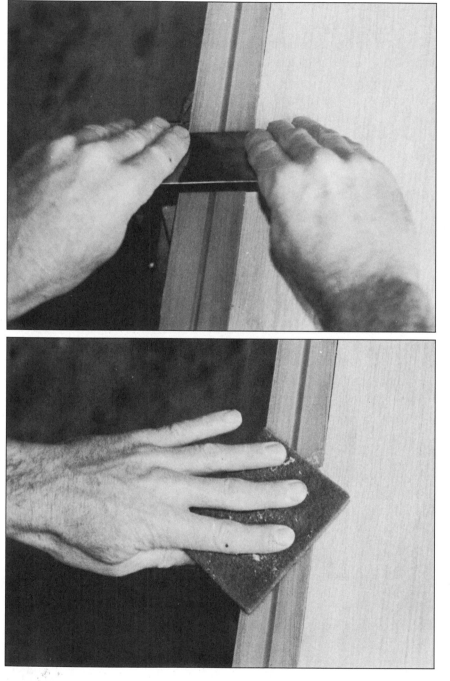

Rilling ski bottoms. First, they are scraped . . .

. . . then smoothed . . .

THE NEW
CROSS-COUNTRY
SKI BOOK

. . . and rilled.

Brushing leads to . . .

WAXING

. . . the finished product.

you don't have a rilling tool, you can use the edge of a file and start at the tip and score the base with those grooves. But don't let any of your Group 4 friends catch you doing this.

After rilling, the base should be brushed clean to get out those plastic fibers, then waxed. So we arrive at the next little difficulty. If you iron in wax, it will fill those grooves you created to allow the water to escape. Correct! So, you put on a light coat of wax and then scrape it gently with a plastic scraper, so as not to destroy the grooves. Then brush it to clean out the rills, or grooves. Or, perhaps better, iron on the lightest coat of wax you can and just brush it. This will probably do a better job of saving the rills, or grooves in your base.

It's a real question if rilling only the tips and tails helps skis waxed with kicker wax under the foot that much. Probably the most important factor affecting speed in this situation is the length and thickness of the kicker wax, not the glider wax you use or the rilling you might do on the tips and tails.

THE NEW
CROSS-COUNTRY
SKI BOOK

Wax Selections

A coaching friend of mine from Sweden, Lennart Strand, and I have been comparing waxing notes for several years. We are two guys who believe in trying to keep things simple and after the last tour we made with the U.S. Ski Team, I wrote him this letter, just to remind him of a joke we had shared.

Dear Lennart,

The other day I went skiing with my wife and as usual, we waxed our own skis the way we wanted to. I rilled the tips and tails of mine, brushed them, melted in a combination of Toko Yellow and Swix Purple glide wax, scraped, then brushed them again. I wanted to try that kicker combination the Team had been using so much, so I ironed on a thin coat of hard green as a binder under the foot, then polished it and followed with my kicker wax. I used two coats each of Swix Special Red and Rex Extra Blue, alternated of course, with the Blue being the last layer. Then I topped it with that Rode Multigrade Blue hardwax.

My wife used Swix Extra Blue and didn't even put on glide wax, but her skis were just as good as mine—maybe faster. She doesn't know as much about waxing as I do. Or, do you think she knows more?

Regards,
John

A Few Variables

If you are skiing with some friends and can switch skis with them, you should learn something about their skis and wax jobs. You might discover that your friend's skis, which have the same wax as yours, just work better. That's the way it is and leads me into a short discussion of the variables in waxing.

WAXING

Let's assume two skiers use the same wax. Will it work the same for both skiers? Probably not. Here are the reasons.

The application may be different. One person might do a good job smoothing the wax and that will work better than a wax job poorly smoothed. Or, one wax thickness may be different and this could make one pair of skis hold better than another.

Skis have different flexes and in general, a stiffer ski will need a bit more kicker wax than a limber ski. But . . . .

Weights vary and a heavier person will be able to flatten his ski easier, thus gaining more purchase than a lightweight. But this same person may be slower using a skating ski waxed full length with glider.

Techniques vary and one skier might sink his weight slightly farther back on the ski than another. Depending on where the kicker wax is located, this will cause different reactions.

The moral is this: learn how to make adjustments in your wax job so the skis work the way you want them to. If they slip, add some more thickness. If they still slip, try a longer wax strip. If they continue to slip, maybe you better try the next softest wax. If that wax slips, add thickness, and so on.

This system usually works, but I remember a night race in West Germany back in 1968 when it didn't. We arrived at the site and it was pretty clear that a cold green wax was just what the doctor ordered. We tried it and it worked for about five minutes, but then it started to warm up. We thickened it, then we lengthened it. Then we tried the next warmest wax and it worked for about five minutes. Second verse, same as the first. Finally, no luck. So we tried the next one, and so on, for 20–30 minutes. After a bit, we fell behind by one whole wax and the race started. What a disaster! The only consolation was that all the other skiers were in the same boat. It was one of those evenings when the warm winds came in and changed things dramatically.

Summary

As I have hinted throughout this chapter, you can go as far as you want with waxing. Some skiers and coaches thrive on new waxes and new methods and every year brings something to delight them. Others want the most efficient wax job they can get and that would be one that is fairly easy to apply, works, and does not depend on having a fairly obscure wax.

Presently, I don't belong to any of the four groups because I am using up what looks like a five year wax supply from my cellar. But I am partial to the methods of the third group because it is the most efficient way to wax in over 90% of the cases I have encountered. I've been waxing for about 40 years and it's relatively easy for me. If you're beginning and want to wax, start in Group 2 and go on from there.

7

Training

BYSTANDERS used to think we were nuts when we trained for skiing. Running along the roads when you could drive a car? What foolishness was this? That was a long time ago and we didn't even train that hard either.

Since the '50s there has been a growing awareness of fitness, and training for whatever you like is quite socially accepted now. In fact, many of the less active people feel a bit out of it and some even write humorous books or tracts on the advantages of a sedentary life. My father-in-law prided himself on the notion that the most exercise he ever got was from peeling bananas.

I never thought seriously of training for x-c skiing until after two years at college. Before that I trained mainly because I enjoyed exercising with the rest of the gang that was out for the team. I also thought it would help my other skiing events, slalom, downhill, and jumping.

After college, Al Merrill and I both turned to teaching and coaching (four events) and used to run into each other on that New England High School circuit. We were both trying out for the Olympic team in 1951, and our training schedule looked like this: teaching every week-day except when we were off with our teams at races, and then tryout races on Saturday and Sunday. We'd meet after the school races and travel to the competition site and try to get some rest. After the last event on Sunday, we'd pack up and make a three or four hour drive home, prepare lessons for the next Monday, and begin all over. That's what was expected—the Puritan ethic, you know.

120

Even summer training eluded me continually. Soon after I had been named to the 1952 Olympic Team in the spring of 1951, I had to serve two years in the Navy. When I was at sea, the best thing I could do was sit-ups and pull-ups and running in place. But at least I ate a lot and kept my weight up! I simply didn't know any better. I didn't have a coach to prod me and there was precious little information on training.

However, I did know about not smoking. In Oslo, during February of 1952, when I saw one of the Norwegian Olympic combined skiers, a mean, strong-looking fellow named Simon Slattvik, sitting in the grandstand a few days before our event watching the jumpers and puffing on a cigarette, I just laughed to myself. Oh boy, was this guy going to be sorry when I skied by him on the x-c course! Well, he beat me by 20 minutes in that race and also won the combined event. Later, after I was told that he was a railroad engineer, I figured he must have been the guy who turned the engines around, by lifting them off the tracks. It also occurred to me that there might have been some elements lacking in my own training program.

When I went to college in the late '40s, a lot of us skied ourselves into shape during the winter. This year-round training stuff was not in vogue. Later on, during the mid-'60s, when I began coaching the U.S. Team, we often had training camps during the Labor Day holidays. Even then, our training camp was the kick-off for some of our top athletes. It's no wonder our results were not too impressive.

About a year after I began coaching the U.S. Team, I scheduled a couple of summer training sessions in an effort to get in some more training and build a little esprit among team members. At the first one, during the summer of 1969, we took a hike, just walking, in order to get in better shape. We started in Vermont at the Canadian border and hiked the Long Trail to Massachusetts, 270 miles away. It took us a bit more than nine days and we averaged about 30 miles a day, over some pretty good terrain. I gaze with fondness at some of the pictures of us at the end of the hike. We looked a bit like prisoners of war at the end of a long death march. But if you compare our results in the 1970 World Championships with previous results, you will see that they were much improved. Something helped and I

United States X-C Team pauses on Mt. Abraham during 1969 Long Trail hike. Left to right: Ned Gillette, Mike Gallagher, Tom Corbin, Everett Dunklee, the author, Peter Davis, Jack Lufkin, Bob Gray, Mike Elliott.

keep thinking it was that little walk. I know I never trained so intensively before or after.

The next summer I scheduled a bike trip around New England. In those days it was considered quite a feat to do 100 miles a day and so we took an eight day trip, 100 miles a day. Towards the end of the trip, after the skiers learned to ride in formation, we would knock off the workout in a bit more than four hours. I felt it was too easy.

But we had a few memorable highlights along the way, not the least of which was the last day when Mike Gallagher joined the parade outside Rutland, Vermont. At the time, Mike was our number one skier and the regulars, who had already been at it for seven days and were feeling a bit mean, cocky, and crusty, were anxious to get hold of Mike in this last workout. Earlier in the summer, Mike had pooh-poohed the use of bikes with racing tires, saying that one could get just as good training with balloon tires, or even touring tires. He may have been right, but the troops did not appreciate his deprecating remarks and resolved to drop Mike and his training tires enroute.

We stopped for lunch outside Manchester, Vermont, and were resting up for the final leg to Putney, the sauna, and some liquid refreshment. Towards the end of the break, Mike got up to go to the john and by prior arrangement, all the other bikers, including Martha Rockwell, who was our best ladies' skier, jumped on their bikes and casually rode out of the parking lot. They did not want to appear to be in a hurry in the event Mike saw them leaving. But the minute they got out of sight around the first corner, they put the hammer down. It was my job to delay Mike for a minute or two extra.

The first part of that afternoon trip was tough, going up Route 30 to the top of the hill outside Manchester. The stronger bikers helped to push the slower ones and the whole group got to the top of the pass considerably ahead of Mike. From there, it was all over, because when a bunch of practiced riders gets up a head of steam, it is very difficult for an individual to catch them. Nevertheless, Mike did his best and the problem was that he had his head down when he finally went by the shortcut to Putney across the covered bridge. He missed it and had to bike an extra eight miles to get to the finish. By the time he got to sauna, everyone was pretty relaxed and you have never heard such hazing in your life. Mike's car was there with his vanity plates, XC 1, and a couple of the guys got some marking pens and changed that to XC 10, figuring that was his ranking after the bike trip.

I thought, poor Mike, this will be hard on him. But, there's a sequel to this story. That September, at our regular Labor Day camp, Mike arrived quite ready for the first workout — which was three time trials on a fairly rugged three mile road run. I seeded the skiers in an interval start, running Mike last because he was the best runner. He passed just about everyone and set a course record, sprinted across the finish, and took off his shoes and walked barefooted past me smiling. "Racing shoes," he said. He had worn his thin-soled track shoes for the first trial. He didn't have to say anything to anyone else.

At the end of these September camps, we often had a few contests that pitted the coaches against the athletes. Since the coaches made up the agenda, you can be sure we stacked the deck. Marty Hall, presently head coach in Canada, was then a good sprinter and so we had a 100 yard dash, which Marty would win. Then we would throw something else at the athletes to give Marty a chance to catch his breath for the 200 yard dash, which he would also win. In the name of coordination, we had tennis matches and it was a snap for me to beat the likes of Mike Elliott and Ned Gillette, thus piling up

Eero Mantyranta, one of Finland's great skiers, getting ready for a spin on some of the first roller skis available to the public. Today's models have dispensed with the skis and simply use a short platform to mount the wheels on.

THE NEW
CROSS-COUNTRY
SKI BOOK

more points for the coaches. It was a fun way to end the camp and it did put some emphasis on events not often associated with x-c skiing. It added variety. Besides that, we coaches always won.

I think one of the valuable lessons we learned from these two summer camps was that the human body has a tremendous capacity for exercise and for learning, if it is brought on gradually. That's the key—building gradually. We tried to. The skiers knew in plenty of time what the plans were and most of them began to train for the camps.

During the same period, a friend of mine, Eric Barradale, and I decided to train for and enter the Vasaloppet, Sweden's biggest ski race. We set a goal of hiking and running from Mt. Snow to that sauna in Putney for our last workout in the fall. We figured if we could do that, we could come close to skiing the 85 km Vasa route.

We began by taking long walks and jogging intermittently, increasing our distances each outing. Eventually the date for the big workout arrived. We stashed food along the backroads on our drive to the start, got out of the car, and took off. We simply followed a scout's method of covering ground and that was to jog, or run for five minutes, then walk for five. After about six miles, I came down with a strange muscle pull in my lower leg, something I had never experienced before. I didn't know what to do, sat down near a pay phone, and was all ready to call home for help, when it went away. We continued and at the end of the hike-run, we both felt rather exhilarated. Thirty-five miles over some rugged terrain—not bad for a couple of middle-aged guys. (We did go to the Vasa and skied the course with unexpected ease.)

These days most casual racers train more, or at least more wisely than we did. There is a wealth of information available for the competitor and it is not my point to get into too much of that programming here. If you want to train for competition, you should get hold of more extensive material. Meanwhile, I'll go over some of the most important aspects of any training program, which include a commitment, that check-up, variety of exercise, the cardio-vascular system along with intensity and pulse rates, strength training, and stretches.

TRAINING

To Begin with—A Commitment

If you want to enjoy your skiing more, it's a good idea to get some exercise during the offseason. If you don't like to call it training, for fear some will think you too serious, identify the exercise as part of your particular lifestyle. That's an in thing to talk about these days. People often tell me I have a good lifestyle, but I don't think they are alluding to my exercise program alone. It is not overwhelming!

On the other hand, you definitely should not feel that large amounts of exercise are necessary before skiing x-c. You can walk off the street and start x-c skiing, as long as you approach it sensibly and go a little bit at a time. I hope you'd take a sensible approach for any new physical activity. In fact, I have listed some precautions below that would apply especially for first-time skiers.

If you're going to get started on some kind of training program, the most important thing you can do is make a time commitment. It doesn't matter how long that commitment is, or what you do at first. But you need to get in the habit of scheduling time for exercise and then go on from there. For some, the commitment might be several hours a week, for others, as little as one hour a week. Save that time, even if you use it just thinking about skiing!

The Check-up

You should check with a doctor before you embark on any physical exercise program. If you've had a family doctor for a number of years, you are in luck because that person will have a history on you and can give good advice. If you're middle-aged (as usual, I refuse to put numbers with this category), and have any history of heart trouble in your family, you should ask your doctor about the feasibility of a stress test.

Variety vs Specificity

I love a variety of exercises and am convinced that it is not absolutely necessary to do ski-related, or specificity exercises, when training for casual skiing. So many things, including physical labor, will help tune you up. I can't think of any games, or sports, that don't have some ruboff value for skiing. Unfortunately, the case for serious racers seems to be different.

The Dilemma for Racers

An interesting situation has occurred with the U.S. Ski Team and it's also becoming more apparent on every level of x-c skiing in this country. For the past few seasons, the U.S. Team has neglected the classical technique and results in these races against the Europeans show it. Some college circuits, at this writing, do not have any classical races on their schedule. Most beginning high school skiers spend the vast majority of their time skating and not doing classical.

However, it's very doubtful the International Ski Federation will give up classical skiing. It's here to stay, and for our racers to train for.

When the word gets out — just about the same time as the publication of this book — that competitors need to train and practice more at the classical techniques, one obvious solution will be to do more roller skiing during the summer and fall. This is specificity training best exemplified. And the competitors won't want to give up skating, or freestyle, so they will have to do some roller blading during the summer and fall as well. With these requirements it will cut way back on the variety of exercising they can do.

Hill-bounding with poles.

TRAINING

Classical skiing offers more opportunities for varietal training than freestyle, or skating. Roller skiing is the most obvious specific exercise, but even running and hill-bounding have some connection with classical. Ski-walking with poles, or without poles, is a good one. Leg bands can be used here too.

Until now, biking has generally been accepted by coaches as good training for skating and classical since it builds up the quadriceps of the legs, but it isn't really specificity training. While high leg tempo is very important for racers and may be developed by biking and using those lower gears to spin a lot, anyone will admit that roller skating or skiing is better and so the emphasis in serious training will be away from the variety that biking offers.

It's possible to improvise and use some inner tubes from bike tires as leg bands and go through the skating motions with these. But aside from roller skating, and leg bands, there isn't much else that will suffice for the best skating training.

That's too bad because in the careers of most long term competitors, many reach a point where the workouts become mechanical and the athletes are often just striving to get in those miles, or hours of training. The quality and varieties of the workouts begin to go out the window, skiers get stale, or bored, and lose the effectiveness of their program. It's at this point that a change is in order, but if the serious competitors are hung up on their specificity training, they'll end up between a rock and a hard place.

There is this important mental aspect to any kind of training. If you are enjoying it and are eager to get out there for your routine, you are doing something right. If it becomes drudgery, or an unwelcome duty you feel you must accomplish, it's probably time for a change in that routine, or time for a rest. A variety of exercises will delay this downer.

For the Tourskiers

For us, it's important to get in a variety of exercises and enjoy life, instead of worrying about being so specific in our training. There are so many great things to do in the summer and fall, like hiking,

One hardly thinks of training when hiking in territory like the Jutenheim of Norway.

running, biking, and rowing, that it would be shameful to neglect them. Then, when the snow comes, we can work on our techniques, choosing the days according to snow conditions.

For instance, when the waxing is difficult, or the conditions are slick and greasy, it's a good time to practice skating. You don't have that waxing problem then. On the other hand, when you can rub on a bit of blue or green hardwax and ski classical on packed powder, there's nothing quite like it, so these are the days to ski classical.

The Cardio-vascular System

Developing a good cardio-vascular system has been highly touted by a lot of doctors. You can see it's a rage by observing the number of books written on training and the wealth of aerobics classes.

Aerobic training is just another term used for cardio-vascular training. It's the meat and potatoes of any decent training program. There are no fancy shortcuts. If you are the slightest bit serious about training for x-c, you have to develop your cv system and that means training for extended periods at elevated pulse rates. (See below for more details on pulse rates.)

The most common methods of training include walking (yes, walking!), walking with poles, hiking with or without poles, jogging, running, biking, rowing, and roller skiing or skating. One of the main ideas of this kind of training is to use a lot of muscle mass. The goal is to build your endurance. You can do some endurance training for your arm by flexing it for a couple of hours but it won't do that much for your cv system. You've got to put more muscles to work than that.

One development with the advent of skating is that many coaches feel less cardio-vascular conditioning is needed, but more strength building and explosive type training, or interval training, is the order of the day. This makes it nice for any of us who want to work on the Nautilus a couple of times a week, or split wood, or play soccer and run a lot of sprints. We can still take those long, easy bike rides, or runs, or rows on the river, or swims, or hikes, or aerobics sessions . . . for the cv system, you know. But now I'm right back to a variety of exercises. Go with it, if it's possible. Lawn mowing is still OK as long as you use a push mower.

The Intensity

The intensity you exercise at is very important. For the casual skier, there is little need to work so hard that you can't carry on a conversation with a friend. When we used to train and came running up the hills, we tried to maintain the same speed as on the flat. The results were pulse rates around 200, all the time. That's crazy. We went too hard, even for serious competitors.

If you are jogging along at a comfortable pace and come to a hill, you had better break into a slow walk or else you will be pushing too hard. If you want to test this out, get hold of a pulse rate monitor and check it during various phases of your exercise. The standard pulse rate of 120 a minute has been established for many years and it's a pretty good guide for a lot of people. You'll be well over this rate jogging an uphill.

An edict, handed down to me from the Bill Bowerman family, is to go with the pattern of easy day, harder day, easy day, harder day.

Three Training Schedules

Here are three training programs, two from opposite ends of the spectrum and my own, rather loosely structured one. Each is set up for the off-snow season in the northern hemisphere. The first program is for someone beginning an exercise program aimed at skiing x-c and the second one is prescribed for a serious college ski racer. Then, there's mine! Hah!

Beginning Schedule

April Walk one mile 2× a week. Do some stretches before and after. Begin to establish a routine.

May Walk one mile 2× a week, one-half mile 2× a week. If this seems easy after two weeks, pick up the pace a bit, but not the distance.

June Walk one mile 2× a week, one-half mile 2× a week, but at an increased pace over your starting pace in May. Take part in some week-end physical activity, such as hiking.

July Walk one and a half miles 2× a week, one mile 2× a week. If this seems easy after two weeks, intersperse walking with jogging. Continue with some week-end activity.

August Walk one and one-half miles 2× a week at a good pace, or tempo. Jog one mile 2× a week. Don't worry if you can't finish the jog—walk it in. Keep up the week-end activity.

September Jog/walk two miles 2× a week. Jog/walk one mile 2× a week. Your week-end activity might be as long as one to two hours at this stage, but the pace is still slow, around 60% of your maximum pulse rate.

(Continued)

October Jog/walk two and one-half miles 2× a week. Jog/walk one and one-half miles 2× a week. Try for an easy, non-stop, two hour session on the week-ends.

If you prefer to mix in some biking instead of doing all walking and jogging, increase the distances by a multiple of two to three.

College Racer's Schedule

April This month is usually reserved for some R and R.

May Ten 10-second hill sprints 3× a week
Strength workout for legs and upper body 3× a week
2–3 hour hike with poles once a week
Roller ski 2× a week
Roller blade 2× a week
TOTAL: 10 hours a week.

June Same as May, **TOTAL:** 11 hours a week

July Same as June, **TOTAL:** 12 hours a week

August Same as July, **TOTAL:** 13 hours a week

September Same as August with following changes and additions:
Hike once 3–4 hours a week
Begin easy intervals 2× a week
TOTAL: 14 hours a week

October Same as September but pick up the intervals slightly
TOTAL: 14 hours a week

Note: The hill sprints should not put you in oxygen debt. Walk down the hill after each sprint and wait for complete recovery. These do a wonderful job of developing leg speed and strength. Be sure to stretch and warm up before these sprints, especially during the colder weather.

My Proposed Personal Schedule

April	Biking 3× a week, beginning on the flats with 10 miles a session Sugaring to clean up the season
May	Biking 5× a week, aiming for Tour of the Valley, a 50+ mile cruise Gardening 6–7× a week
June	Biking 3× a week—tours ranging 10–30 miles in hilly terrain Rowing 3× a week, beginning 4 miles a session Gardening as necessary
July	Same as June with rowing increased to 6 miles
August	Same as July
September	Back to work. No biking, but increased intensity rowing 3× a week, aiming for the Green Mountain Head, a 3 mile race Cutting wood 3× a week, gardening
October	Same as September with roller skiing beginning to replace rowing

If you take any exercise designed to improve your physical capacity—and it doesn't matter if it's a short spell of doing something for 15 minutes, or taking a long run of 15 miles—and it ranks as a harder day for you, ease up the next day. Otherwise, you will begin to wear yourself down.

The quality vs quantity aspect is associated with this easy day, hard day plan. Too many people believe in the "no strain, no gain" philosophy. Or, more is better. I believe you should have some mustard left after any exercise bout. Don't end up tearing yourself down and exposing yourself to tiredness, sickness, or injury.

TRAINING

Pulse Rates

If you're more serious about fine-tuning your training, you should read some other books that get into more detail. But, I'll give you a few tips on pulse rates right here.

Many pulse rate recommendations are based on a percentage of your maximum pr. It takes a good warm-up, then quite a stint of exercise, plus a good pr monitor to actually record your max. Even then, lots of people fail to max out or get an accurate reading, for one reason or another. So you can estimate your max pr by using the old formula: subtract your age from 220, and that's close enough.

For an easy distance workout, you should keep your heart rate at 60%–70% of max. For a 60 year old, the computation goes like this: $220 - 60 = 160$ max pr. Then, $60\% \times 160 = 96$, which is the base rate for exercise. The upper limit for an easy workout for this person would be $70\% \times 160$, or 112.

For a 20 year old, the figures work out to 120 and 140 as the limits—for an easy workout.

Intensities can be increased, of course, but as the intensity increases, the time spent exercising should decrease, radically. As I have hinted, there is not much point in the casual skier exercising beyond this easy distance range. And a lot of racers would be well-off to spend at least 80% of their time in this range.

Anaerobic Threshold

Eventually, a lot of skiers want to go a bit harder, or try to get in better shape quicker. The term anaerobic threshold then pops up. This is the point in your exercise where your body systems go from primarily an aerobic situation (roughly speaking, if you are exercising aerobically, you are able to provide all the oxygen you need by breathing) to what's called an anaerobic one. Anaerobic means without oxygen, and of course you have some oxygen coming into the system when you stress yourself, but there isn't enough of it and you begin to feel cramped, or fuzzy, or get paresthesias.

So what? How many times have you heard the person who says he could have gone faster at something but he ran out of breath?

Chances are that his anaerobic threshold was low and most certainly that he crossed over his threshold. One present member of the U.S. Team was measured and found to have his threshold at a pulse rate of 155. This means that as soon as he exercises at a level that takes his pulse above 155, he begins to operate anaerobically, or put another popular way, he runs into oxygen debt. How much better if his threshold was at 165 or 170!

Now you get it. The point in serious training is to raise your threshold rate. The problem is how to do it.

First, you have to find your threshold. Here's another formula that gives you a figure that isn't too far off. Multiply your max pr by 85% and you have it.

If our 60 year old wants to work on his threshold—although I don't recommend it—he should flirt with a pulse rate of 136. The 20 year old will have to get up there around 170!

Some coaches think that exercising just below and just above the threshold rate will raise that level. But there are an increasing number of coaches who think that exercising at much lower pr levels will also raise your threshold. Since this is the more conservative approach, I would tend to go with it. You can do a few selected bouts at your threshold, or above, but don't carry on too long.

If you're at all serious about measuring your pulse rate, you should get a pr monitor. Taking your pulse by feeling your wrist, or your neck, after exercise is not really accurate enough. Sometimes it's hard to record, or count the beats, since there are fluctuations when you stop exercising. These will throw off the true value of your exercise rate.

Strength

With more racers and tougher courses, there's no question that strength training is a very important ingredient of any serious competitor's program. For the rest of us, I would recommend a lowkey approach to this aspect of training. Too much time spent in the weight room deprives a person of the opportunity to do something more pleasurable out-of-doors. If training time is scarce, you might as well enjoy it to the fullest.

Homemade roller board and dip machine in Caldwell's outdoor gym.

Don't worry. If you do any exercise with regularity, you're going to get stronger at it. If you want to continue to improve your strength, you can begin to overload a bit. If you're hiking, carry a weighted pack. If you're running, you can wear one of those weighted vests, or run up the hills a bit more. If you're biking, throw in some more uphills. If you're rowing, pull harder for some stretches. For roller skating or skiing, just try more uphills.

During any of these increased periods of intensity, pay attention to your body and your pulse rate. Don't overdo it and strain a muscle, or get your pulse near maximum. At this stage it's not worth risking anything like this.

Precautions

For even the most casual exerciser, there are some precautions you can take and a lot of little bits of knowledge that will help you. I've made a lot of mistakes during my career and maybe you can learn from some of them.

The doctor, Stan James, once told me that about 90% of exercise-related injuries, from muscle pulls and strains to the more traumatic stuff, were a result of a change in routine. Say you've built up a nice biking routine and it gets too cold for that. You decide to start running and go out the first day and knock off several miles. A mistake! Your legs are probably not ready for it and you will end up with sore muscles, or worse.

I remember a Putney student who got in good shape during the ski season and went home to the city for spring vacation. He began running and called me to tell me he was averaging 10 miles a day, after four days! Said he felt just great, and he did because his cv system was probably at peak. A few days later, he strained the ligaments in his knees and had to rest several weeks before he could start in running again.

In 1952, just prior to the Olympics, I was bopping around the streets of Hanover, New Hampshire, where we had gone for a meet. I was in good skiing shape but got excited by being back in my college town and ran a bit, ending up with a bad case of shin splints. I hadn't done any running for a couple of months and those hard streets did the trick. Luckily, my doctor, Si Dunklee, was along on the trip and he gave me daily rubdowns to help ease the pain.

Joint Workouts and Stretches

Now, when I start any new exercise routine, I begin with what I call joint workouts. Rarely do I work up a sweat, but simply begin to familiarize my joints with this new movement. It could be splitting wood, rowing, biking, even hoeing in the garden. I've been lamed up too often to do otherwise. I do these joint exercises for a week and begin to supplement them with a bunch of stretching exercises. I can tell when my body is adjusting.

The skating technique seems to put more stress on various joints than classical skiing and if you're going to skate, you would be well-advised to do a lot of preparatory exercises for the legs, and hips especially. Soccer stretches are good, with emphasis on the groin muscles and hips. Some work with the leg bands would be helpful too.

Speaking of groin stretches, don't forget to do them for classical skiing in the beginning of the year. Few regular track skiers have survived on those hard, fast tracks without some strain in the early season. If only they had done more stretches!

Roller Skiing and Skating

If you're more serious about specificity training, you can get roller skis or roller blades (skates) and strike off on the roads. Now, here's a place where you must be careful because there have been some fatal accidents from skiers colliding with motor vehicles. Be sure you are always in control and always on the side of the road. If you haven't used these contraptions before, start slowly with about 10–15 minutes a day during times when the roads are not busy. I can't really recommend these to you unless you are training for racing.

Vintage picture. Coach Caldwell surveys Mike Gallagher and his "new" roller skis.

Special Events

Many people who ski x-c engage in all sorts of events during the offseason, mainly because they are fun and expose them to different people and different sports.

Charlie Kellogg, a former U.S. Olympic skier, got together with a bunch of footrunners to train for the Sedan Chair Race when he was working in Hong Kong. It's a benefit for the Matilda Hospital and in this one a team of eight has the job of carrying a person—usually a small one—in a sedan chair from the Matilda Hospital on Mt. Kellett down toward the Star Peak tram and back up again. It's a distance of well over two miles, round trip.

The teams work in shifts of six. Two members jog along and rest, then relieve two of the carriers. The passes are similar in importance to a baton pass in a relay race.

The year Charlie organized the team, he found that having runners with the same stride length and same reach, or size, was an important factor and took this into account when making up the team. It paid off and his team won.

TRAINING

The Sedan Chair Race is a big event and usually has about 40 entries. The streets on the course are blocked off and thousands of spectators watch the proceedings. There are several winners—judged on time, attire, attraction to the crowd, amount of sponsorships, and so on.

Events like the Sedan Chair Race are different and offer a change to the normal modes of exercising. Some are historical events and help provide plenty of inspiration throughout the rest of the year. Anyone can get good ideas by engaging in unusual contests and carry them over into their own sport, or community.

Hong Kong also has a Dragon Boat Race Festival each year and this international event attracts over 100 boats, or war canoes, from around the world. Some boats have as many as 23 paddlers aboard. In addition to the international event, there are several local events where villages, or colonies, sponsor boats of their own and race each other. It's a very colorful event and just another example of something exciting that almost anyone can enjoy.

Triathlons are very popular around here and three person teams can be fun, as long as no one gets too serious. Most skiers can find a triathlon where they can take a leg. The best part of these events may be the business afterward, the talking about it, the meeting of other participants, and the wondering how it will go in another year. Now, if I just go a little faster on that section there. . . .

My Birkebeiner buddy, Skip Sheldon, introduced me to rowing several years ago. (I had dabbled in the '50s when I was in college, but that was short-lived.) On a visit to Long Island, Skip put me in his ocean shell and I immediately ordered my own to use on the Connecticut River at home. Since then, another friend, George Heller, has spearheaded the growth of rowing in this area and early each fall a bunch of us sponsor the Green Mountain Head, a stake race of three miles on the river. Last year we had about 100 entrants. It's the idea of rowing in the Head that keeps many of us training during the summer.

You don't have to be an aspiring Olympian to go in any of these events like a triathlon, a rowing race, or any other contest. Participation is the most important ingredient.

If you live in an area where you can't get out into the country easily and take hikes, runs, and bike rides, you still have several options. Many fitness centers have rowing machines, treadmills, bike machines, and even those x-c machines. Don't ignore squash and handball, indoor tennis, swimming, weight workouts, aerobics with a group, or any other forms of exercise that can be had in populated areas. In a way, there is a larger variety of offerings in the city than in the country.

8

The Fun of It

*I*N THE early days of x-c skiing in the states, there was not much fun associated with it. The sport was practiced by relatively few people, nearly 100% males, and it wasn't considered a major form of recreation.

The most famous skier of the early days was John "Snowshoe" Thompson who, during the mid-1800s, accomplished many amazing feats on skis. For example, he routinely carried mail from Placerville, California, to Genoa, now in Nevada, during the winter months. This called for skiing about 90 miles over the Sierra Nevada Mountains during all sorts of weather. Much has been written about his exploits and Snowshoe even had a U.S. commemorative postage stamp published in his honor. But it was many years before skiing got established as a sport in the United States.

The Scandinavians brought the sport to the states and in a few small communities there was some skiing—primarily what we would call downhill skiing now—and some ski-jumping. When the third Winter Olympics were held in Lake Placid in 1932, the United States had a small team for the x-c events and another one for the 1936 Games in Germany. Unfortunately, World War II intervened and the next two Olympics were cancelled. Finally, at the 1948 Olympics, the United States got into international competition on a regular basis.

During the 1940s and 1950s, several colleges and high schools began skiing x-c competitively and this constituted a very high percentage—probably well over 90%—of all x-c done in the states. In 1950 the United States hosted the World Championships in the

Nordic events and its existence was a secret worthy of the CIA. But there were more international events abroad during the '50s and this meant more teams and more competitors. When the Olympics were again held in the United States in 1960, at Squaw Valley, California, a lot of people began to take notice of x-c.

In short, the history of competitive x-c skiing prior to 1950 is pretty sparse. But the history of recreational x-c is even thinner than that and nothing much happened until the 1960s. So it's a fairly new sport in this country.

X-C Ski Areas

There has been a lack of tradition of going skiing at x-c areas. I know lots of people who skied Alpine at Suicide Six in Woodstock, Vermont, in the '30s, and I started skiing there and at places like Stowe in the '40s. The growth of Alpine areas has been notable since the '50s, but it wasn't until the '70s that x-c areas really got going.

Today there are over 800 x-c areas and they provide skiers with well-groomed trails, lessons, rentals, and often food and beverage services.

Just as it makes sense to begin tennis on a decent court, so it makes sense to start skiing where it's easiest. Set tracks make the steering of skis much easier, and packed snow makes skating easier as well. You wouldn't want to start learning tennis on a court full of bumps and stones, would you?

Trail design has changed from the early days when trails were similar to goat paths. Now they are wider and have fewer abrupt changes in direction and pitch—all this to accommodate higher speeds and better equipment. Snow compaction has progressed from the days of using snowshoes, or x-c skis, to the use of machines and in some cases, tillers behind the machines. This makes the snow more uniform and easier to wax for. These are the conditions beginners need in order to best learn all the basics.

Rentals are especially useful if you want to try out different skis before buying your own. If you find the right area, you will have a large choice of different skis, and some places have special sales of rentals at the season's end.

The food and beverage service is another plus, even if you are a brownbagger. There's no telling when you will need some extra snacks.

Some areas have overnight accommodations as well. You can make these places the destination for a week-end or a week's vacation, or more.

Trail Etiquette

The combination of increased numbers of x-c skiers and the new skating technique demands that we all be more alert and considerate when we ski, especially at areas open to the public.

In general, it's customary to ski on the right side of the trail. This allows overtaking skiers to pass on the left, as in driving cars on the road.

Given this basic approach, a couple of other procedures follow.

Sometimes the snow groomers will put a track on the right side of the trail, leaving the rest of the width of the trail for skaters. If you are skating, for goodness' sake, don't ruin the tracks set for the classical skiers.

If you are skiing around a trail and see the track set on the left, there is a good chance you are going the wrong way. (A few areas have trails that are bidirectional, but the trend is away from these since they increase the chance of head-ons.) Turn around and get going in the right direction.

If you are skiing up a hill and see there are a lot of straight, parallel tracks instead of herring-bone tracks, there are only two possibilities: first, you're going the wrong way again or, second, everyone ahead of you had super wax on and went straight up the hill. (A very unlikely situation!)

When you find a place with parallel tracks, don't use two

Skating on tracked snow—a no-no.

sets of them by overlapping. Leave room for other skiers. Simply stay right.

If you are skiing side by side with some skiers, be alert to others who may want to go by.

If you fall on a downhill, don't spend too much time lying there feeling sorry for yourself because someone else may come wheeling down on top of you.

If you ever got your pole basket or ski tip stuck in a footprint hole, or spent much time grooming snow, you'd never leave footprints on the track yourself.

I've mentioned littering and taking dogs along elsewhere. Simply put, please don't!

THE FUN OF IT

Many Alpine areas like Stratton have touring centers adjacent to the mountain.

In short, x-c ski areas are getting more and more service oriented. Gone are the days when you drove to the end of a road somewhere and skied out to an open shelter and called this going to a ski area. Now the challenge for the areas would seem to be to make their trails as exciting and manageable as possible. Short downhills with banked corners, rolls in the terrain like a roller coaster, good views, and parallel tracks will all enhance the sport.

Instruction

For a few years, when x-c was growing rapidly, a bunch of promotions came out saying, in effect, that if you can walk, you can ski x-c. Since then the wiser heads have withdrawn that statement. Many instructors found people who indeed could walk but just had an awful time trying to learn to ski. In addition, most ski instructors don't like to think of x-c skiing as walking on skis. That omits the basic thrill of the sport, which is called gliding. (That's all Alpine skiers do during the day—they glide downhill on skis.) The basic technique any x-c instructor looks for, whether it's classical or skating, is the glide. Does the skier glide?

When skiers glide they are skiing more efficiently and can therefore cover more terrain. It's also relaxing and thrilling to glide and this adds to the pleasures of x-c skiing. There's nothing quite like skiing abreast of friends in double, triple, or quadruple parallel tracks, and talking about any topic of your choosing. When you are out cruising, you should be able to hold a conversation—that's one of the guidelines for pleasurable skiing.

For beginners it's a good idea to take multiple lessons. After one or two lessons, you may be able to get along moderately well on the easy terrain, but you might be developing some bad habits that could be corrected by another lesson. Or, you might be ready for the next steps in your learning experience. The better you get, the easier it is.

A family picnic at the touring area in Waterville Valley, New Hampshire.

THE FUN OF IT

Winter Camping

There is lots of good information available on winter camping and I'm not going into that. I don't feel qualified besides. I know there are some types who consider anyone a no one unless he has done the winter camping bit and so I want to recount a few of my experiences, just to be part of the club.

When I was in the eighth grade at Putney School, we went off to a meet at Pico Peak that Karl Acker had pulled together. There were three events. One was slalom, one was jumping, and the other was an Alpine technique event where we were asked to execute various maneuvers like the stem turn and the snowplow. It was a lot of fun and after the meet, our coach, John Holden, said, "OK gang, now we're going to the cabin to make supper and spend the night." I envisioned some heated, comfortable cabin with electricity, toilets, the whole bit.

We drove up to the pass where the Long Trail crosses the road, jumped out, grabbed our gear, and started wading through this hip-deep snow toward a cabin somewhere off the trail. When we got there, we found the door was partially open since the snow drift had blocked it that way. The sides of the cabin were made of small logs with spaces between that one could look through. The fireplace was big and when we got a fire going, it created a great draft, right up the chimney. By the time we got around to cooking supper, much of the food had frozen and we took the obvious route to survival and climbed in our sleeping bags for the night.

Well, that was 1941. Things got better.

In 1945, while I was still at Putney, we went to the state ski championships at Stowe. Sepp Rupsch set a slalom for us on the slalom glade on the Nose Dive. When the event dragged on towards late afternoon, we knew our fate. The lifts had stopped running. In true Putney fashion, we were camping out on this meet too. I don't know at the time whether it was meant to be a punishment for those interested in athletics or it was part of the school philosophy. Maybe the school was broke and couldn't afford to buy us rooms. Anyway, we were staying in the Stone Hut just over the knoll from the top of the chair lift. We did have the foresight to stow our packs and sleeping bags there before the race, but here we were halfway down the mountain, tired from racing, and it was getting dark. There was no choice. We climbed up the mountain and stayed the night.

This hut was much tighter than the one at Pico, but if you've ever tried to heat a stone hut near the top of a mountain during windy, cold weather, you know what we were in for. Rink Earle was our coach then and he wasn't enjoying the evening much more than we were, but he kept us laughing with a lot of good stories.

Just a few years ago, John Stookey organized a January winter camping and skiing trip on the Allagash River in Maine. He had heard of people canoeing down the Allagash and thought it would be something different for a group to ski down the river. He invited me along to act as chief waxer. We also had a doctor, a photographer, a college president, and two Putney students in tow. We flew into the headwaters area with all our gear and when that plane took off, I felt as isolated as I ever have. We settled down for the night in the vicinity of a few summer cabins. I slept on the porch of one and for once in the winter, was warm. Well, considering I had a new, five pound down bag, I should have been. When I woke up, I noticed the temperature was 19°F below zero. Nice nippy day to get started.

We managed to ski along the river for several miles each day, carrying packs, tents, food, and anything else we might need. But while we skied, we had to try and make good time in order to reach our destination because we had made just one mistake in our planning. We didn't realize the amount of

(Continued)

time it would take to get organized every morning in subzero temperatures. There were certain things you had to do with your bare hands, like open packages, tie up ski boots, pack bags, and so on. Off with the gloves for as long as you could stand it, then on with the gloves while you warmed your hands. In the afternoons, if we didn't stop by 3 P.M., we found ourselves groping around in the dark trying to make supper, or clean up before bedtime, which usually came around 7 P.M.

I certainly enjoyed this trip and can say, there, I've done that. My present inclination is to be able to use more daylight for skiing, then retire to a heated building for the evening. But I still take at least two non-snow camping trips a year, one in the spring and the other in the fall.

The Organized Tour—A Tour Race

Many people get turned off by racing and often it's just a frame of mind that causes this. One of the best tours you can take is that where you pay an entry fee, wear a bib to identify yourself, line up with a lot of other skiers, and strike off for your destination. I call it a controlled tour.

The course has been mapped and prepared for skiing. You'll find good company along the way; food stations, and first aid people will be available. It takes a lot of that preparation worry off your shoulders. All you have to do is pretend you are out for a tour.

I've had a blast on some of these tours. When I went in the Vasaloppet in 1968, there were quite a few companions—over 10,000, I guess. But there were four parallel tracks for the first 50 km, plus a bunch of food stations. I will admit that when the track offerings narrowed to two at the 50 km mark, many of us started going faster. In physics it's a well-known phenomenon that water flowing through a large pipe will go much faster if it is channelled into a smaller pipe and this is exactly what happened to us. For the next 15 km, I don't think I ever skied faster in my life. As a result, when I got to the food station at 65 km, I had "run out of groceries." I was in sugar debt. I took the food offered there and sat down on a bench behind the tables to recover.

Before the race I had planned everything and had some extra wax, a cork, and a few small items of clothing—all nested in the big front pocket of my jacket-top. Being a bit foggy, all I could think of was jettisoning extra weight, like an airplane low on gas and looking for a place to land, so I started spilling that equipment on the ground behind me. A couple of youngsters ran over and asked if I was sure I didn't want these things. With a wave of my hand, it was clear they could have them. At that point I didn't care what happened.

It took only a few minutes to recover and after I took another drink from the food table, I got back with the traffic and started going pretty well. Near the 80 km mark, just a few km from the end, a friendly skier came alongside and began asking questions, in Swedish. I pretended to understand him and grunted, "Ja," in answer to the first few questions, but finally when he asked one and looked at me quizzically, I had to admit that I didn't understand Swedish. He said that was OK, then he would speak to me in English. By this time I was beginning to stagger again and really didn't feel like talking, but he persisted and soon it became apparent to him that I was quite tired. He whipped out a couple of dextrose tablets and handed them to me. I plopped them in my mouth and chewed them. But, being dehydrated, I had difficulty salivating enough to swallow that ground-up powder. It was just like chalk dust. I choked a bit, coughed it down, and when he saw I was all set, he sailed away, wishing me good luck. I'll never forget that fellow. I saw him briefly at the finish and he acknowledged me with a nod. For him it was just one of those normal occurrences during a tour.

That was a fine tour, Salen to Mora. Eric Barradale, who also made the tour, and I met our wives along with our goodfriends the Greenes, and celebrated with a dinner in town that night afterwards. We were on an exercise high the rest of the evening.

The organizers sent me a certificate showing my time and place of finish and I bought one of those pictures they take of you some-

THE FUN OF IT

One of the "food" stops in the 1986 Pub-to-Pub Classic, Perisher Valley, Australia.

where along the course. These mementos help to recall that day.

Here's another tour for you. It suits me fine because I think I've found an event I can be competitive in . . . at last.

A few years ago, some of the x-c skiers and ski patrolmen were sitting around a bar at Perisher Valley, Australia. The day was over and they were comparing notes and teasing each other, as usual. The question of skiing and drinking beer fast came up. The patrolmen allowed as how they could hit a few of the bars in the Valley, take the T-bars up the slope to make connections to the other bars by skiing, and beat the knickers off the x-c'ers, who would naturally ski from bar to bar without benefit of uphill facilities. A contest was born and three patrolmen and three x-c skiers battled it out the first year.

The next year the race was opened up and there were 50 competitors, the next year 150, and last year, 250 competitors. One wag suggested that this might soon become the largest race in the southern hemisphere and perhaps they should apply for an FIS sanction, even though it's only a 5 km distance.

The Swan Brewing Company took on the sponsorship and gave it a name, the Pub-to-Pub Classic. Four person teams, which must include both sexes, are featured. Gaudy uniforms have already become a part of the Classic tradition.

Now the race starts at the Smiggins Ski Area, just about 1 km downhill from most of the bars in Perisher Valley. The contestants line up at the start, beer in hand, drink it down at the start signal, and head toward Perisher. They make four stops at the outdoor bars set up there, drinking a beer at each before heading on to the next "food station." After that, it's back down the hill to Smiggins, off with the skis, rush inside, and—you guessed it—drink another beer before checking in at the finish table.

Where else but Australia?

There are all sorts of tours in between the Vasa and the Pub-to-Pub Classic and it isn't hard to find one that will suit you.

False Starts

Starting methods differ at these tours. You can never tell what is going to happen and you have to be alert in order to avoid getting trampled.

At a Washington's Birthday Tour we ran at Putney one year, I

Start of the Birkebeiner in Norway. Each skier is required to carry an 11 pound pack.

THE FUN OF IT

Starting section of Washington's Birthday Tour, 1972, and on facing page, the 1987 version. The techniques have changed.

thought we should put on a typical Vermont scene. I arranged for Stuart Simonds, the owner of the property where the start was, to come out with his shotgun and fire it to start the race. I had a stopwatch synchronized with the master clock at the finish 20 km away, so Stuart and I took our position about 100 feet in front of the 1200 racers who were waiting for the signal. I turned my back to the racers because I didn't want them to see me giving any signals to the starter. Then I gave the countdown, quietly. "Five-4-3-2-1-Go," I said. "Click," went the shotgun. It had misfired. A few of the eager skiers in the front ranks heard the click and took off. Almost immediately, most of the others took off, but at that time, Stuart, realizing the shell had misfired, pulled out a pistol he had in reserve. It was very good of him to think of this eventuality, but in his excitement he fired the pistol twice. The skiers with a background in track racing took that signal as a recall and pulled up short. But the other skiers didn't know any better and kept on coming. The track people almost got run over, realized the situation, and took off again. It was too late to restart and we let them go. It all worked out, but it was a panic for a while.

In another instance, at the Vasa in 1968, the start time was listed

for 7:45 A.M. The organizers had positioned 200 elite skiers in front of the pack—the pack being another 10,000 skiers split into two groups—and about 7:35 a few of the skiers in the second rank of about 3000 made a move. Then a few more jumped and finally the whole group broke and was surging forward. The elite bunch heard this noise, looked over their shoulders, and took off like scared rabbits. Of course, the rear echelon of over 7000 began to move too, and it became a case of 10,000 skiers jumping the gun . . . by 10 minutes!

Question! You're the organizer. What do you do? I guess if you're wise, you stand back.

Flexible Situations

Some tours in the past have worked on the honor system. You show up sometime in the morning presumably, jot down your time of departure, ski the course to the end, and make a note of your time. The organizers collect the time sheets, make the calculations, and send results to those interested.

You can probably find a tour where they encourage you to take along a picnic and a camera and to make stops on the way. You can also surely find those where almost everyone seems to be in a hurry. (Some people call it a race.)

If you take any one of these tours, you will probably remember it for a long time. You might get hooked and decide on some more tours. It's a nice way to go when the organizers do so much for you.

THE FUN OF IT

Dogs

Lots of photographs show people skiing x-c with a dog happily (presumably) bounding alongside. What typical family is there without a dog to go to the country with? Nixon was the first president I recall who had an association with dogs. Ever since his TV appearance, a lot of people have been buying dogfood.

We too have a dog, but he never goes skiing with us. It's not really cricket when you realize all the problems. I won't get into the notions of how dogs feel when they are wading through snow, or how they feel when they are left behind while the rest of the family goes off on a pleasurable jaunt. A lot of this thinking is conjecture.

But, dogs usually make prints, or holes in the snow, which can catch a ski tip or pole basket. They can easily obliterate fresh tracks. They pose a danger to skiers who are trying to ski by them, or who come upon them on a fast downhill section. Hitting a dog while skiing is not good for the dog, the skier, or the owners of the dog. Then there are the dog reminders they leave on the trails. Have you ever seen a dog traipse off into the deep snow to unload?

Finally, and this is a danger not many people think about, dogs come upon wild animals, and particularly deer, by following ski trails through the woods. Most wild animals are fighting for survival during the winter and are in weakened conditions, unable to outrun dogs, or dogpacks. What follows is simply brutal and something no one can condone. Wild animals in these conditions are no match for well-rested, well-fed dogs.

Leave Rover at home, or in the car, when you go skiing.

A winter triathlon scene involving running, skiing, and biking.

On Your Own

There are still plenty of people who like to strike out on their own, forgoing packed trails, x-c areas, tours, or anything that smacks of organization. Most of them are plenty rugged and know what they can handle. They may prefer being alone, or object to the idea of paying a fee for skiing. I'm part of this group at times and I know the feeling.

The best times I have had skiing x-c have been taking tours, especially from one location to another—something involving extra transportation by car or bus to the start, or from the destination back home. I just get a kick out of skiing to a destination as compared to skiing around a big loop. But that's my preference. I get home and look at the map again to see where I've been and give a sigh of satisfaction. Does this sound corny? I can't help it. It's the truth!

THE FUN OF IT

The Ski Is on the Other Foot Now

When Ski-Doos first hit the market, they caused an immediate conflict with the x-c skiers. (The word "Ski-Doo" is a brand name for a machine made by the Bombadier Company, but it has become a popular generic term to use for all snow machines of this type.) Owners of the machines quickly took to the trails that many x-c skiers had considered their own. One pass of a machine often ruined any tracks that had been set or skied in. The machines made noise and in general were not welcomed by many skiers.

But, to their credit, the Ski-Doo people soon got organized, charged licensing fees, and used the income to lobby for more areas to use their machines in. They began organizing clubs and reasonable procedures for behavior. In our area we talked with the local club and explained our situation with respect to x-c trails and had no problems. In fact, the Ski-Doo club helped us to pack the x-c trail for a big touring race we ran in Putney in 1972.

Some hard feeling remained in other sections when the machine people and the x-c people ran into each other. I suppose it will continue. Recently however, a lot of skiers have caught on to the trails that the Ski-Dooers use and are having a ball skiing them. Many areas have groomers for their Ski-Doo trails and when they finish you can't find many better places for skating. Classical works OK here too. The trails, being mostly in wilderness areas, are beautiful and I can recommend your trying them sometime.

Now, the Ski-Dooers are doing the skiers a big favor. Be nice to them.

With the Kids

I may have gotten my preference for destination tours from experiences with our own kids. As soon as they turned two, or had learned to ski, they were eligible for a trip my wife and I used to take with regularity. It started outside our kitchen door and went down a logging road for about half a km. Then there was a small climb followed by more level and downhill terrain. The trek went on for about 2 km and at the end of it, my wife or I would be waiting in the car to drive them home. The car ride took a fair time because it was about 5 km back. So the kids always got the feeling they had really made a long trip. It was easy and helped them to gain confidence in skiing.

I think many of us fail to realize what little kids like, or what impresses them, and we make a mistake in trying to engage them in adult-like activities. If you throw a bunch of kids together on x-c skis and watch them to see what happens, you might be surprised. They are quite adventurous and considerate. They'll usually help one

THE FUN OF IT

The Pied Piper.

another, think up games to play, run around on skis falling all over the place just for fun, build little snow jumps to ride off, play follow-the-leader, or challenge each other to short races.

If kids are put in a situation where they have to follow adults, say, on a tour, it can get tedious for them because they don't feel they can match the grown-ups. On the other hand, offer the same trip to a bunch of kids, with perhaps one adult tagging along, and chances are they will eat it up. We used to let our kids lead and explore along the way on our little tours. Or, we would be looking for a lunch spot somewhere and ask them to search one out for us. It's good if you can make it their game.

Food and Other Considerations

For long tours around here, we take along high energy food like chocolate, cheese and Triscuits, and liquids—I quit drinking out of the streams since giardia became so popular—and enough warm clothing to wear in the event of a weather change, or to keep warm when we might have to wait for a ride back home. This is a pretty simple situation. We can ski for miles and miles and not cross any roads, but on the other hand, we are never far from civilization and

THE NEW
CROSS-COUNTRY
SKI BOOK

in the event of a mishap, we would not have a hard time finding help. This is not the case everywhere everyone takes tours and so before you go out, you might imagine the "worst possible scenario" and act accordingly. It never hurts to take extra precautions. And I couldn't possibly prescribe them all here, for each section of the country. However, here are a few suggestions.

In general, if you go out on an extended tour of a couple hours, or more, you should take all the same precautions you would climbing some mountains for the same period of time. If you've had experience doing these kind of trips, you're all set. If you haven't had experience, you should go along with someone who has. Failing these two situations, be sure to heed any good advice you can get.

You should know about the worst weather that can befall you and prepare for it. Every year I read about hunters who get stranded in their cabins due to heavy snows somewhere in the west. Most of these hunters have jeeps or four-wheel-drive vehicles that you would think they could drive out. They can't *all* be taking a little extra, "forced" vacation. I wonder what would happen to me if I got stuck skiing in weather like that. Not good!

A group of three is a minimum. Figure it out. If something happened to one member and you needed help, it would be best if one person stayed with the incapacitated while another went for help.

Take enough food and liquid to last you an extra meal, in the event you need it.

Take enough extra clothing, like windbreakers, hats, socks, and gloves, to take care of you if your trip is delayed until after dark.

Don't go so fast in the early stages that you sweat profusely and soak all your clothing. If you begin to perspire a lot, slow down, or shed some clothes, or do both. Wet clothes are not so comfortable when you get cold. And by perspiring you lose extra liquids that you might need later on.

It's always good to take a route you know has been traversed before. At least you know it comes out. Take maps at any rate.

Be sure everyone in your group is in good enough physical shape and has done something like this before. Long ski tours are not for the physically unfit. Set a pace that is comfortable for the slowest

THE FUN OF IT

member of the group. This way there is much less chance of anyone running into sugar debt, or becoming physically exhausted.

Don't underestimate the energy it takes to cope with being out-of-doors in the cold, breaking tracks through deep snow, and trying to cover even a relatively short distance of 10 km.

Before snowmobiles came in, I was packing one of our x-c courses with snowshoes one day. It was a simple 5 km loop and I went around it once with no problem. I needed to do it twice and started out, got about 2 km, and ran out of groceries. I had no energy left, felt woozy, and the trees had stopped going by so fast. Luckily, I was just about 100 m from a road that went by my house. I staggered out to the road, just barely made it up over the big snowbank, slid

Jack Rabbitt

There is no way I could finish this book without telling you my favorite experience with Jack Rabbitt Johanssen. Jack Rabbitt has been given all sorts of deserved credit for helping to establish cross-country skiing in Canada. From his earliest days on this continent, he was a legend, and remained so until he died recently going on the age of 112.

Back in the late '40s, when I was skiing the college carnival circuit at Dartmouth, we went to a meet north of Montreal, sponsored by McGill. The cross-country course had been laid out by this fellow named Jack Rabbitt, someone I had never heard of, but who soon gained my respect, as well as that of many others.

It happened that one skier in the x-c race missed a turn about 1 km from the finish and came skiing through from the wrong direction. There was much consternation until this lean and craggy, crusty-looking, 74 year old Jack Rabbitt was consulted. He got hold of the racer and said, "C'mon, we'll go out to the point where you went wrong and look it over." They did and we all stood around wondering what was going to happen. Soon, the two of them appeared, skiing like crazy, but coming from different directions. The racer finished the way he had during the race and Jack Rabbitt skied in, wearing his rucksack, on the correct course. They arrived together and while the racer was catching his breath, Jack Rabbitt said, "See, it's very simple. He didn't lose any time and he didn't gain any time. The distances are the same."

None of us doubted Jack Rabbitt. But, the people who knew him figured the racer got the better of the deal since he probably couldn't ski as fast as Jack Rabbitt.

down the other side of it headfirst onto the road's surface, and lay there exhausted, snowshoes dangling at odd angles above me on the bank. What a sight! After a while a car came by, picked me up, and drove me home, which was a whopping 300 m away. I got some food into my stomach and was OK, almost instantly. But I didn't have the food out there on the trail and apparently was already in a weakened condition, or very tired when I started out and didn't realize it.

The Landowners

You often hear pleas for respecting the landowners, whether you hike, hunt, or ski on others' property. The reasons are pretty clear and most people would not think of starting fires without permission, or leaving trash lying about after a picnic. But I think it's great if you can go that extra step and make the landowners respect you as a skier. Search them out to thank them. You might come across a situation where you could help them out with a mere 5 or 10 minutes' work shovelling snow, or carrying and stacking some wood, or pushing out a vehicle. I can guarantee you the landowners will never forget experiences like this. And neither will you.

In Sum

Cross-country skiing is still a sport where you get the most enjoyment from simply going out and doing it. Don't forget it. Don't let the so-called advances of the electronic age beguile you and take away the simplest pleasures in all of skiing. If you get too hung up on the latest equipment, or the newest method for preparing your ski bottoms, you're going to miss a lot of action on the trails. Many x-c'ers take a certain pride in their independence by ignoring innovations.

I spend a certain amount of time being a maverick and I love to listen to serious discussions on skis' qualities, the proper flexes and sidecamber, the fastest bases and tip designs, and all that sort of stuff. If anyone asks me what I think, I tell them to make sure the curved part is out front. That's the most important thing to look for when you put on your skis.

There are lots of new theories on training and the best clothing to wear. The latest waxes always demand a lot of attention from racers and it gets passed on to other, less serious skiers. I'm waiting for some computer software that will program skiers for about anything they want to do. Most of this stuff misses the point, or detracts from the enjoyment of skiing. If you're enjoying yourself skiing now, beware the latest advance. Study it for a couple of years to see if it's still around. Then, if it's convenient, try it out.

Meanwhile, go skiing. Have fun.

Index